SIGNS
AND WONDERS

Firsthand Experiences
of Healing

St. Andrew Convent
1992

SIGNS AND WONDERS

Firsthand Experiences of Healing

—◆—

Fr. Ralph A. DiOrio

IMAGE BOOKS
Doubleday
New York
1987

Library of Congress Cataloging-in-Publication Data

DiOrio, Ralph A., 1930–

  Signs and wonders.

  1. Spiritual healing—Case studies. 2. Miracles—
Case studies. 3. DiOrio, Ralph A., 1930–
I. Title.
BT732.5.D57   1987   234′.13   87-6697

This Image Book Original published October 1987 by special ar-
rangement with the Apostolate of Prayer for Healing Evangelism,
Worcester, Massachusetts

Scriptural citations in this book are from The Living Bible, Para-
phrased, Catholic Edition, copyright © 1971 by Tyndale House
Publishers, Wheaton, Illinois; New American Standard Bible, copyright © 1960 by the Lockman Foundation for Creation House Inc.,
Carol Stream, Illinois; The Holy Bible, Revised Standard Edition,
copyright © 1982 by Holman Bible Publishers for Cokesbury.

To my mother, Molly, whose guidance and inspiration, prayers and dedication, have been a mainstay in my whole life and in my service to the Lord . . . with deep love and respect and gratitude

ACKNOWLEDGMENTS

May the Holy Spirit fill the lives of each person who glorifies God by sharing a miracle through this book.

I am also deeply grateful to my staff at the Apostolate of Prayer for Healing and Evangelism for their perpetual assistance and support. My co-workers and I offer special thanks to Jeanne B. Carter, R.N., who compiled and verified the cases.

Above all, credit is due Jean Laquidara Hill, who edited this book for publication. Her skill and professional expertise in writing and re-writing have made her a valuable asset to my ministry.

CONTENTS

INTRODUCTION

Many years ago, as the story goes, a man named Jesus walked the earth spreading love, and ridding His Father's children of illness and disease. These miracles, or signs and wonders as they are also called, not only restored health but also turned doubters toward God.

Accounts of the miracles spread from household to household by word of mouth. The populated world was smaller then, and it was practical for Jesus to walk about healing people one by one. He still heals individuals as they walk along the road, suffer alone in their hospital beds, or reach out for comfort through a prayer-line call. Sometimes, however, perhaps because of the multitudinous population and the need for mass witnessing of miracles, Jesus heals God's children publicly through a mortal; even a humble, simple priest such as me.

The people He heals inevitably spread the word in supermarkets, in restaurants, at church, over coffee, while jogging, and through books such as this one. Their purpose is not to draw attention to themselves, but rather to focus your attention on God's love for each and every one of us.

You will meet some of these people here. They are loved by God no more or less than you or I. If there is something visually distinctive about all these people it is that they all are happy and at ease with themselves and their Lord, God. You see, a healing accomplishes more than the repair of a mortal, human body or mind, it transforms forever a person's relationship with God. No matter how strong that relationship was to begin with, no matter how faithful and close to God the healed person was, the experience of healing places that relationship on an entirely new plane. God becomes more real, more tangible.

For those who doubt God's existence or compassion to begin with, a healing opens the door for the first time to a mutual communion. The association exists from the beginning, even for those who consider themselves faithless, because God loves all His children from the beginning. I believe every person has at least a speck of hope that God exists, and therefore a speck of faith. I do not believe, however, that God doles out healings on the basis of faith, and therefore I call neither Him nor myself a faith healer.

Jesus, the Divine Physician, out of His compassion and love for us, knows our needs, hears our calls, and heals. I am simply a conduit through which He sends His healing love. Why or how God chose me, I do not know, but I sincerely thank Him and accept His will for me. I also cannot tell you why or how God selects who or what illness He will and will not heal, except that He does not base the decision on the amount of the person's faith.

I also know that He is a loving God who does not strike His children down with sickness. He does, however, sometimes use that illness to bring His children back to Him, to walk with Him for all their days and rest with Him for all eternity. In His infinite wisdom and love, God knows our greatest joy comes from being with Him now and forever. That is why He sent His Son to teach us to be fishers of men, as we are told in Matthew, chapter 4, verses 19–23:

> And He said to them, "Follow Me, and I will make you fishers of men." And they immediately left their nets, and followed Him.

*And going on from there He saw two other brothers,
James the son of Zebedee, and John his brother, in
the boat with Zebedee their father, mending their
nets; and He called them.*

*And they immediately left the boat and their father,
and followed Him.*

*And Jesus was going about in all Galilee, teaching
in their synagogues, and proclaiming the gospel of
the kingdom, and healing every kind of disease and
every kind of sickness among the people.*

Further on in Matthew we are reminded that
Jesus gave His apostles authority over illness and sent
them to teach and heal.

*And having summoned His twelve disciples, He gave
them authority over unclean spirits, to cast them
out, and to heal every kind of disease and every
kind of sickness.*

(Matthew 10:1)

Divine intervention is not an alternative to medical intervention. Often, as you will read in these reports, God and doctors work hand in hand. Physicians, some of whom attend my healing services, often
welcome God as partner in their medical practices.
Physicians, particularly those who recognize the importance of holistic healing, have some of the same
concerns as I: the healing of the mind, body, and
spirit. Of course, our areas of specialization differ.

If you have not attended one of my healing services, you may be curious about what happens there.
Many of your questions will be answered by the testi-
monies on these pages, but I will clarify a few matters.
First, let me stress once again that I heal no one. God

heals. I have no power and want no glory. I am a priest.

My services are held most often in very large facilities such as auditoriums or Madison Square Garden to accommodate as many of God's children as possible. I preach God's word, lead people in prayer and praise, and bless and anoint the people who attend, and sometimes, by proxy, those who cannot be there.

Every step I take, I take with Jesus. I take my direction from God, through prayer and reading the Bible.

> *And he told them, "You are to go into the world and preach the Good News to everyone, everywhere."*

> *(Mark 16:15)*

> *When the Lord was finished talking with them, he was taken up into heaven and sat down at God's right hand.*

> *And the disciples went everywhere preaching, and the Lord was with them and confirmed what they said by the miracles that followed their messages.*

> *(Mark 16:19–20)*

While I am teaching and worshipping, I am under the anointing of the Holy Spirit and experience various healing insights. Sometimes I will call out a general healing of the eyes or ears and I will ask those in need to stand, and I will lead the congregation in prayer. Afterward, everyone who has been healed is asked to come forward and claim the healing.

> *Is anyone among you suffering? Let him pray. Is anyone cheerful? Let him sing praises.*

Is anyone among you sick? Let him call the elders of the church, and let them pray over him, anointing him with oil in the name of the Lord; and the prayer offered in faith will restore the one who is sick, and the Lord will raise him up, and if he has committed sins, they will be forgiven him.

(James 5:13–15)

At other times during a session I will get a feeling that someone in a particular area has a specific need. I also experience the Word of Knowledge, and call out a person with a certain name, color of clothing, or disease. I am led by the Holy Spirit to identify exactly the illness, need, person, or a combination of these. Frequently I call these people to me and pray over them. A person does not need to be called out or touched by me to be healed. Often, however, I will walk among the people and anoint them with blessed oil or bless them with holy water. Depending on the size of the crowd and the time at hand, I may bless every person individually or bless the masses by sprinkling, using the holy water as a point of contact.

While being prayed over, blessed, or just being in the presence of the Holy Spirit at the sessions, a person may fall over, or pass out to rest with the Holy Spirit. This is called being slain in the Spirit. At times, entire rows of people fall down like dominoes. Never is anyone injured when truly slain in the Spirit. The experience varies, with some being in a state of altered consciousness and others being totally unaware of what is happening around them. While some expect to be slain, others are shocked, but happy. Some cry uncontrollably, releasing tears of healing, but many simply smile the warm, content smile of a beloved child of God. Leading someone to rest in the Spirit is part of the gift of healing, a direct touching of the innermost being by an infilling of God's love and peace.

Not everyone who is called to be healed is asking for the gift of health. In fact, many who are given the gift attend the services on behalf of another whose pain they compassionately feel. Others head for the services to pray for their own intentions, but once they arrive their attention is diverted to the pain and suffering of others. There are those, too, who come only to praise Jesus, through Whose pain and suffering they are saved. They lay their prayers at the foot of the cross and cry that Jesus suffered so, and that God loved them enough to sacrifice His Son.

> *For God loved the world so much that he gave his only Son that anyone who believes in him shall not perish but have eternal life. God did not send his son into the world to condemn it, but to save it.*
>
> *(John 3:16–17)*

Some of God's children attend services simply to feel closer to Him, or to pray that they may forgive others and be forgiven.

You will meet some of these people here. Let me introduce Barbara MacRae, who turned to God suddenly because of impending death. Now she spends her life in service to the Lord. You also will meet others, some of whom stumbled across God, and others, such as Roger Berube, who first tried other painkillers, then tried God.

You will get to know Dorothy Sullivan, a vibrant mother of seven, who withstood incomprehensible anguish until God healed her; and Louis Marino, whose parents tearfully prayed that he be made well.

You will meet a delightful little girl, Sarah Pesto, who gladly and without hesitation accepted her gift of health from her Maker, and Dr. Barrera, who was willing to accept health from God but once doubted my gift. The accounts in these pages are told by people who have shared various versions of unique experiences. Some of them have never met anyone else who experienced anything similar, yet they step out in faith, their heads held high, and report their innermost feelings to you. For this I sincerely offer my heartfelt appreciation.

The healings reported here are true. The staff at the Apostolate of Prayer for Healing and Evangelism documents each case, substantiates each testimony, and obtains medical records to ensure both truth and accuracy. I offer these accounts that you may be aware that God truly loves you and that you are never alone. I pray that you have faith in God, and that these accounts help affirm that faith. I pray that you know God, and that through these accounts you get to know Him more personally. For me, I ask only that you never confuse the facts. God heals. I do not. I work quietly, prayerfully, gratefully, for the glory of God and the winning of souls, with no motives in between.

It is my prayer that you get to know each of the persons who speaks to you through this book. Feel their pain and experience their boundless joy. Have compassion for them and for any person who hurts in any way. Open your heart to God and His children.

AUTHOR'S NOTE

As of this writing the following presentations indicate that through divine and medical intervention positive changes have occurred. As is appropriately noted in the stories, some illnesses require specific or minimum periods of time before they can be considered completely healed.

"Have Mercy on My Child"

Louis Marino
New York, New York

Healing: Myelofibrosis

Then Jesus told him, "Go back home. Your son is healed!" And the man believed Jesus and started home. While he was on his way, some of his servants met him with the news that all was well—his son had recovered. He asked them when the lad had begun to feel better, and they replied, "Yesterday afternoon at about one o'clock his fever suddenly disappeared!" Then the father realized it was the same moment that Jesus had told him, "Your son is healed." And the officer and his entire household believed that he was Jesus. (John 4:50–53)

On September 18, 1982, Maria and Louie Marino's fourth baby, Louis, was born. Once again God had blessed the Marinos with a healthy child. A happy baby, Louis delighted his family with gurgles and smiles. Mrs. Marino tended to her son's every need, lovingly, carefully. She fed him, bathed him, cuddled him, and kept him safe. It is up to the parents, after all, to keep a baby well. Sometimes, however, the best parenting in the world is not enough. A horrible illness over which parents have no control can, and occasionally does, strip health from a tiny child. That is what happened to Louis, as Maria recalls.

On March 14, when Louis was six months old, he was a happy, healthy baby. I put him to bed as usual that night. When he awoke he had a nosebleed and a fever, so I took him to the doctor. Louis looked very pale, and the doctor ordered blood tests.

Louis was admitted to the hospital for more tests. After four days we were told that our baby had a rare, dangerous disease called myelofibrosis. Only twenty children in the United States had ever been diagnosed with this disease, and nineteen of those children had died. In children who have myelofibrosis, their bone marrow produces a powderlike substance instead of blood platelets. While a normal blood platelet count is 150,000 to 400,000, Louis's count was 11,000. The doctor was amazed that baby Louis was alive with such a low platelet count, and said Louis could easily have bled to death.

There is no known cure for myelofibrosis. Medically, Louis's only hope was for a bone-marrow transplant, an experimental procedure which had never been attempted on a baby.

After two weeks Louis was released from the hospital, but I had to bring him back three times a week for blood transfusions and tests. There was little hope that Louis would survive, and we were frightened. Louis's doctors told us not to take our baby anyplace where groups of people gathered, such as on a bus or to a party. We were told to keep him at home except for short walks and hospital appointments.

For personal reasons, my husband and I had stayed away from the church for some time, and our relationship with God was not the strong bond it is now. Fortunately, a friend of ours brought a very prayerful woman, Nancy, to our house to help us pray for our son. For years we had seen her wearing a neck brace, but after visiting Father Ralph A. DiOrio, she no longer needed it. She had been healed. Through Nancy we realized the unconditional love God feels for us. Spiritually, this was a beautiful time of growth for my husband, Louie, and me. We returned to church, and Louie and his father reconciled their differences. We were shown how much love there is in the world. People from all walks of life, who did not even know us, offered their prayers, support, and assistance to us and our child. During this time Nancy brought us to see Father Peter McCall weekly to pray for our baby.

Everything happened in rapid succession. In April, only one month after we were given the tragic news about Louis, my husband, Louie, went to a service held by Father DiOrio. Our baby was in the hospital at the time. Louie was so elated when he returned home that I was sure Father had called out that our son was healed. I was wrong, however. It was hard for my husband to relate his experience to me at that time. I did not understand completely. Louie said he felt happy because so many people were healed at the service. Something else happened. It seemed so simple to me, but it had affected Louie very deeply. As Father walked down the aisle, he touched my husband's sleeve and said, "Believe and have faith in God."

Meanwhile, baby Louis was released from the hospital, and I continued taking him to the hospital for blood transfusions and tests. He was not getting any better, and I had become desperate. Although we were not supposed to take Louis into groups, I sent for tickets to Father DiOrio's May 15 service in Manhattan College. The auditorium holds four thousand people. To make matters riskier, it was raining that day, and we stood in the rain for almost an hour before the doors opened.

I sat in the front row holding my baby. Louie and our other son sat about ten rows behind us because the front seats were reserved for the very ill. About twenty minutes after Father DiOrio entered the room, the baby started to scream and sweat. He became very wet. I tried to calm him, but an usher came over to me and said that perhaps Louis was being healed. Father never called on me that day, but the service was wonderful, and I cried for the entire six hours we were there.

The next day, Father DiOrio telephoned us at our home and offered to meet with us. He came and prayed over Louis with my husband, my mother-in-law, and me. After prayer, Father told us gently that it was all in God's hands now.

The hospital blood tests I have forwarded to the Apostolate of Prayer tell the rest of the story. Tests taken in March and April clearly show Louis's low platelet count. Three days after Father prayed with us, the platelets had doubled! From that day on, our baby's platelet count continued to increase until July, when it became normal.

Now, in the fall of 1986, Louis is four years old and only needs annual checkups. He is a healthy, happy boy who enjoys his family, including his new little sister.

PRAYER

Dear Father in heaven, You will never be outdone in Your unconditional love for us, Your children. I am very much aware of Your love. Through the experiences life thrusts upon us, You introduce us to new spiritual growth. Souls are Your business. Soul-winning costs You so much. It cost You the price of pain for Your beloved Son when He was sacrificed on Calvary. How noble You make us and how well You sustain us.

Through the healing of my son Louis, You made the world's spiritual perspective crystal clear.

I take this moment to thank You, dear Father in heaven, for reinforcing the fact that life is precious and filled with gifts from a heavenly God who wants to be in touch with us.

In this moment of sincere prayer, I thank You for healing the world's deep despair.

"An Easier Life"

Dorothy Sullivan
Butte, Montana

Healing: Phlebitis

". . . And send your healing power, and may miracles and wonders be done by the name of your holy servant Jesus." (Acts 4:30)

Dottie Sullivan, a mother and grandmother, is a vibrant woman who exudes the enthusiasm and energy of a perky teenager. She seems not at all like a woman who spent more than twenty years fighting an uphill battle against phlebitis. A painful inflammation of the veins, phlebitis interferes with blood circulation and can cause blood clots. Think about what Dottie's life must have been like, spending month after month in the hospital after losing one leg, only to fall and render the other useless. Now try to imagine her as a young woman enduring operation after operation, year after year, and spending so much time in the hospital that she ached to be with her seven children. This is how her life was until she submitted to the ultimate remedy. Read on as she tells you the whole story.

More than twenty years ago, when my sixth and seventh children were born, the doctor decided I should have the veins in my leg stripped. I had phlebitis and had spent six weeks in the hospital prior to the birth of my twins. After the vein surgery, I never was able to put my foot on the floor again. My leg was white and cold, with blisters as large as baseballs. It had swelled to three times its normal size, popping the stitches open. The doctors put ice packs on my leg, then stitched it back up in my bed. From then on, it was downhill. I spent the next two months in the hospital suffering in extreme pain. My twins were premature and had spent six weeks in the hospital while I was there, but I had been moved to another floor and couldn't see them. After two months, my husband asked the doctor if I had gangrene, which is a rotting away of tissue. When the doctor answered yes, my husband demanded that I be transferred to Providence Hospital in Seattle, Washington. My foot had turned black. It was rotting away from the ankle and sloughing away from the calf. I had holes in my leg draining off fluid. When I left Butte I thought I never would see my kids again. I thought I was going to die.

The surgeon at Providence Hospital was a dear Christian man who said he believed that God guided his hand as he operated. When he looked at my leg in the operating room, he was shocked. He just couldn't believe it. He walked over and stood by the window for about twenty minutes. I guess he didn't know how to break it to me. When he came back over to me, he said my leg had no blood supply and needed to be removed as soon as possible. I was not sure I could go through with it, so he said he would conduct more tests to confirm a lack of blood supply. The next morning an arteriography was conducted to see if any blood was flowing through my leg. The diagnosis was confirmed. My lower leg had no blood supply. I gave permission and the surgeon cut off my foot, ankle, and part of my lower leg.

Because I was given such high doses of morphine and other drugs at the hospital in Butte, my doctor said he could not risk giving me any pain medication after the amputation. The pain was awful.

As my doctor explained, the doctors in the first hospital had mistakenly tied off the major blood supply to my leg. That was why it had infected and rotted. The amputation saved my life. After the amputation, I had surgery thirteen times over several months. I never cried. I never felt sorry for myself, but I had seven children at home ranging from infancy to eight years old and I was concerned for them. After about six months, I started to cry because I missed my kids so much.

Eventually, I was fitted for a prosthesis, taught to

get around, and allowed to go home to my husband and children. I had been in the hospital from January until September. Unfortunately, problems developed six weeks after my homecoming and I was forced back into the hospital. A second amputation was performed to remove what remained of my lower leg below the knee. Finally, I was recovered sufficiently to go home. I spent Christmas in the midst of my family. What a thrill!

Problems with the stump persisted, so my back-and-forth visits to the hospital continued. Meanwhile, my good leg also was being treated for phlebitis. As time went on, I carried out life's daily chores and tended to my children's needs as well as I could.

Sometime later, I tripped over our dog's bone and fell down the stairs, injuring my good leg, my only leg. Blood clots formed near the ankle. Leg problems continued relentlessly while my children were growing up, but I got around.

By October 1983, when I first considered attending one of Father DiOrio's healing services in Butte, Montana, my oldest children were grown and my daughter had just had a baby. Instead of attending the service, I spent the time helping my daughter and enjoying my new grandchild. Then, in February 1984, I heard that Father DiOrio was holding a service in Spokane, Washington. Again I hoped to attend, but unfortunately I was hospitalized for phlebitis in my good leg at the time of the healing service. I began to pray about my situation and decided to call St. Thomas Parish in Spokane. The person in charge of Father DiOrio's services suggested that I come down in early summer, but I had a bad hemorrhage in my good leg and had to stay in the hospital for another ten days. The doctors called in a specialist, who told me there was nothing he could do for me at that time. He told me to stay off my leg. Well, I had been off my leg most of the summer. After all the blood was reabsorbed into my leg, he would conduct a surgical test to determine its condition. Even though it was a minor procedure, I was scared to death because I had blood clots from my ankle to my groin. Well, I prayed about it and thought maybe everything would be okay for me.

I had been listening to Father DiOrio's tapes and had read his books. I said the healing prayer every night and a rosary every night that God would get me to Father DiOrio.

The minor surgical procedure turned out to be major surgery. Carrying out all my chores and running a seven-child household on one leg had taken its toll. Under my kneecap I had a growth as big as a golf ball. All my cartilage was shredded and I had such a bad case of arthritis that the bone had to be scraped. Instead of thirty minutes, the surgery took almost three hours. I emerged from surgery in extreme pain and suffering, and I thought, "How can I ever get to Father DiOrio's service!" This was August 10 and Father DiOrio was scheduled to be in Spokane on August 26.

I had been talking to my husband about Father DiOrio for a long time. I was excited, but he thought I was getting carried away. It was very important to me to attend a healing service. I just had to go. Five days before the service I ended up in the hospital again. Friends and people I didn't even know started coming to visit me. They had heard about my situation and understood how much I wanted to get to Father's service. My husband, doubting the healing ministry and fearful that the trip would land me in an out-of-state hospital, did not want me to go. A fire fighter and my son-in-law each volunteered to drive me to the service, but at the last minute my husband agreed to go with me. I was so happy. In all, nine of us set out on the two-day trek. My leg was packed in ice and I just prayed I would be able to bear the ride. God was really with us. My sister and her husband were with us. My sister prayed that Jesus would lead Father DiOrio to me, but I told her not to have great expectations, that we were very fortunate just to be attending the service.

When the ushers saw me in the wheelchair waiting outside the service, they brought my husband and me in and seated us immediately. The rest of our party waited outside.

The minute I got inside I just had to cry. The choir was singing "How Great Thou Art" and my tears were flowing like a river. I couldn't stop. It was getting embarrassing, so I picked up the service pamphlet and tried to read it. It said, "Do not feel embarrassed if you cry. These are tears of healing." As the music filled the room, I saw Father DiOrio standing near the choir. I got so excited. He just looked to me like one of Christ's apostles. Then he went out of sight and the priests and the bishop filed in carrying the Eucharist. Behind the bishop walked this humble man, Father DiOrio, carrying his rosary. As he came around the corner and walked toward the wheelchair section, he came right over to me and dropped his rosary across my foot. Right away my family became elated. They thought I was healed on the spot, but I wasn't. A short while after Father started the service, he said, "Those in wheelchairs, get up. Feel where the pain is. Touch it. Walk. Get up out of those chairs. Walk."

I felt warm then, but I kept holding back. A little girl with rheumatoid arthritis was healed. It was so thrilling. They were taking her braces off and her mother was so happy that she was babbling on and on. Father smiled and said, "I think you need to go to sleep for a while," and out she went. She was slain in the Spirit. It was just amazing! The little girl was showing everyone her legs and she started laughing at the sight of her mother laid out that way.

There were many healings, then Father came around again. I'll tell you, when you see these miracles —you believe. He repeated, "Those in wheelchairs, get up. Get up. Feel where the pain is. Touch where that pain is." I was feeling it and all of a sudden I just pushed down on the wheelchair lever. I took the packs off my leg, threw them into the chair, and stood up. I was feeling warm and I was in a trance as Father continued working through the crowd. I must have stood there for thirty minutes. Then, all of a sudden, he came up the steps and thanked God and the people for all the special things that had happened that day. Suddenly he turned to me and said, "Well, honey, how do you feel?" I said, "Better." He said, "How do you feel?" I answered, "Wonderful." He said, "Walk to me," and I thought, Walk? I dragged my foot about two steps and he repeated, "Walk to me." I walked about twenty feet. Then he told me to jump up and down. Well, I'm not much of a jumper. I couldn't believe it, but I jumped up and down. He told me to do a little dance and so I did a little dance. I'm not usually one to do this sort of thing in front of people. Next he said, "Push that wheelchair out of there," so I shoved it as though I was mad at it. Then he told me to hug my husband, and I did. My family was crying and I was shouting, "God loves me." Never before would I have shouted in public. God's presence was overwhelming. I just can't explain it.

His power never ends and my faith has no end. Mere words cannot express how grateful I am to our Lord Jesus for shedding His loving mercy on me. I know that God is my personal friend and I face all my difficulties with Him. I have had no problems with my leg since my healing, and there is no sign of phlebitis. I will thank God for the rest of my life. Not only did I have a physical healing but the spiritual healing I had has opened my life to Jesus, our Savior. I know that God is Love.

AUTHOR'S NOTE

Primary physician's note follows:

January 22, 1986

Apostolate of Prayer
for
Healing and Evangelization
761 Main Street
Leicester, Massachusetts 01524

Attention: Jeanne B. Carter, R.N.

Re: Mrs. Dorothy Sullivan

Mrs. Sullivan has been a patient of mine for nearly twenty years. When first seen by me, she had had a below the knee amputation of left leg and had phlebitis in the right leg. Over the years it would be necessary to hospitalize her three to four times per year with the phlebitis and complications of the Coumadin therapy, diuretics, etc. She had to have lab work at least twice a month and be seen in the office for swelling and pain in the right leg and the left stump.

She sprained the right knee and had cartilage injury and a knee full of blood for which she was operated by Dr. Charles Canty.

Since August, 1984, when she was seen by Father DiOrio, she has had no phlebitis or leg problems and her knee is strong and stable. Her leg is soft and non-swollen and non tender and pain free, for all of which there is no medical reason.

Mrs. Sullivan has shown a dramatic turnabout in a twenty year chronic condition and must be considered a healing.

Sincerely,

Daniel E. Staples, M.D.
DES:ro

PRAYER

Lord, I am a living person with human feelings flowing through my veins. It is so unnatural to be anything but whole. How awful it was to relinquish my exuberance to the excruciating inflammation in my legs.

There are times I would reminisce, almost believing I was still a teenager. Every one of us wants to be vibrant and useful. We hate the intrusion of any illness. Sickness is a menace of the evil one. It has no respect for any person, young or old, rich or poor, male or female, adult or child. How horrible disease is! God hates it and He did something about it. He sent His Son to heal us. Thank You, Father. Thank You, Lord Jesus. Your compassion burst apart the sickness which I carried each day for so many years.

I turned to You, dear Father, as a child turns to a parent. You heard me crying. You embraced me and mended me with divine healing. You not only saved my body from decay, but also embel-

lished afresh my soul in a new Baptism of holy
love. Your presence is overwhelming, dear Lord. I
have experienced it. How will I explain it? My
faith, soaked in the experience of Your love, will
never fade. With the vibrancy of my renewed life, I
exuberantly cry out, "Thank You, Lord for Your
mercy, Your concern, Your healing touch!"

"Give Me Proof"

Alberto M. Barrera, M.D.
Niantic, Connecticut

Healing: Coronary artery disease

Jesus looked at them intently, then said, "Without God, it is utterly impossible. But with God everything is possible." (Mark 10:27)

Dr. Alberto M. Barrera is a broad, strong man with a warm heart and a gift for telling a story. Ask him a question about scripture, and he will spend his time explaining his answer to you. He studies the Word, cherishes God, and did not doubt God's ability and desire to perform miracles. You see, Dr. Barrera was a surgeon during the revolution in China, and knows that God guided his hands during surgery, blessing at least two of his patients with miraculous recoveries. Could his faith be stretched large enough to believe that God had made Father DiOrio an instrument of healing? Give me proof, he asked, and God answered.

I am a sixty-eight-year-old general practitioner who has been practicing medicine for forty-five years, fifteen of which were spent in research. Nine years ago, in 1977, I began to have typical angina pain, which is pain in the chest. The cramping took away my breath and moved toward my neck and my left arm. The pain grew increasingly severe. On six occasions I demanded admission to the coronary artery disease intensive care unit of the local hospital and was attended to by my colleagues. Each time I was discharged with a diagnosis of anxiety neurosis, not coronary artery disease.

The coronary arteries, as you may know, are the arteries which circulate around the heart and feed the blood through the heart, which then pumps it through the body. The heart does not steal the blood it is pumping. Like every other organ in the body, the heart must receive oxygenated blood by means of arteries. These arteries that carry nourishment to the heart are called coronary arteries. In coronary artery

disease, the arteries become narrowed, either temporarily by spasms or permanently by deposits of plaque.
The plaque narrows the opening of the tunnels of the
arteries, therefore allowing less blood to flow to the
heart. As the tunnel narrows, the arteries spasm and
cause pain angina. Artery spasms also can be caused
by stress and worry.

Thank goodness I treated myself throughout this
period with nitroglycerin, which opens up, or relaxes,
the spasms of the heart even when the arteries are
filled with plaque. I know the saying is that the doctor
who treats himself has a fool for a patient and an idiot
for a doctor. However, lacking anything better, I did
treat myself. So this went on for some years, until it
became so bad that sometime around January, 1984,
during my seventh admission to the coronary care
unit, I insisted on a thallium scan of my heart. For this
scan, a whitish substance is injected into the blood-
stream, which carries it into the coronary arteries. The
whitish liquid enters the heart, making it appear trans-
lucent. In contrast, areas that do not receive enough
oxygenated blood appear as darkened patches. In this
way, there is physical evidence of whether there is obstruction to the coronary arteries.

Although my colleagues did not agree with my
diagnosis, they agreed to do a thallium scan of my
heart. The dye was injected and in fact showed a darkened area of the heart, therefore proving there was
blockage of the artery. My coronary problems were
caused not by anxiety but by actual obstruction of the
coronary arteries. So, to follow this up, I had an angiogram done on me. An angiogram is performed by in-
jecting dye into a long tube which has been pushed
through the arteries into the heart. The dye can be
seen moving through the arteries. Movies are taken of
this procedure so that, slide by slide, the arteries can
be studied to see where the blockage is. To the doctors'

surprise, but not much to mine, four arteries were found to be 75 percent to 90 percent plugged.

A doctor at Yale who is head of the hospital cardiological department said, "Alberto, this is very serious. When will you be ready to have a bypass operation to direct blood around the blocked area?" That was Friday, and I was operated on on Monday. Because people often wait four to six months for such surgery, I was concerned that some other patient would have to wait while I took his place. But the doctor from Yale said my case was more urgent than others waiting. The surgeons performed four coronary bypasses on me, using vessels removed from my leg. Theoretically, this was supposed to cure the problem. Unfortunately, however, bypasses sometimes close between one and ten years after the operation.

In my case, I had a year and a half of relative freedom from pain before starting a downward course. In January 1985 I was readmitted to the coronary care unit, where I failed the stress test. The stress test is a test in which you ride a bicycle or something to determine how much exertion you can endure before the heart lacks blood. During this test they put the thallium into my blood vessel again, and the result of the scan, unfortunately, was lack of blood to the heart. To understand exactly what had happened, we ran another angiogram, which showed that one of the four bypasses had closed completely. My heart stopped during this test and I was zapped with voltage through chest paddles to start the heart again. In my case, it took five zaps before my heart started again.

So I asked the doctors if they could bypass the blocked bypass artery, but they could not. You see, to do a bypass you need two free ends of the artery, but in my case only one end was open. The only way it could have been done was by inserting a balloon catheter to open the narrowed artery. They declined to do this because they feared my heart would stop beating again. I therefore returned home without any hope of medical treatment.

I had constant, increasing angina despite increasing the medications. I also started taking in oxygen. It helped me breathe, and besides, I had one less artery carrying blood to my heart and assumed increasing my oxygen intake would help provide more oxygenated blood to my heart and help keep me alive. Only one artery needs to be blocked to cause death. I was bedridden for a month and a half. I had to increase the nitroglycerin to dilate my arteries, and the increased dosage caused terrible, intense headaches. I put patches of nitroglycerin on my chest and was taking it by mouth as well. The chest and head pain became so unbearable that I had to take morphine or Demerol for relief. Toward the end, I was having three or four injections of painkillers daily.

So, with oxygen tanks, I went down to see the head cardiologist at Yale again and told him, "You have to help me. I'm going downhill very rapidly and I'm even using morphine or Demerol. Of course, I try to avoid it, but when I can't stand the pain anymore, I do give the shots of morphine." He answered me, "Alberto, don't suffer needless pain. When you have the pain, don't wait for it to get bad. Whenever you have the pain, shoot as much morphine or Demerol as necessary to control it." I asked him, "What are you saying?" and he answered, "You know what I'm saying. You know your own condition. I'm as frustrated as you are, but there is nothing I can do." So I went home to die. There was nothing the hospital could do for me. I had medicines and oxygen at home, and my wife, who is an excellent nurse, gave me nursing care. So I got my affairs in order; sold my stocks, paid off the mortgage on the house, and was waiting for the end. My wife wanted me to go to the hospital, but I

was determined to just die at home. However, one day
after I had already called our priest to give me the
Sacrament of the Sick, my blood pressure fell. My sys-
tolic (contracting) pressure went below ninety. At that
point there is hardly enough blood pressure to support
brain functions. I became semiconscious, and my wife
sent for an ambulance to take me to the hospital. I was
not happy when I regained consciousness and found
myself there. I reproached my wife, telling her I must
go if God is calling me. She said, "God is not calling
you. You are not going to die." Now, my wife is a very
educated person with a very scientific mind and several master's degrees. Well, she told me she was going
to take me to see Father Ralph A. DiOrio, an instrument of healing. I checked up on this Father DiOrio
with priests I know and with our archbishop. I also
asked a state trooper friend of mine to find out about
this man for me. He attended one of Father DiOrio's
services and reported that people were leaving their
wheelchairs and claiming healings. By the way, this
trooper friend of mine does not believe in God. He
said to me, "I don't know how much the church paid
these guys to pretend they were healed." I said, "Oh
no. The church will not pay to have miracles faked.
On the contrary, the church would be very eager to
prevent these things from happening."

I thought to myself, Well, by Jove, there are a lot
of people who think they are sick and who have psy-
chosomatic illnesses who can be cured by hypnotists
and others. I do believe in miracles because I believe
God performed two miracles on my patients during
the war, saving them. I did not, however, believe in
this DiOrio fellow. But, I reasoned, if I don't try him,
when I die my wife may believe that I could have been
saved.

So, with my wife, my son, and five tanks of oxygen, I set out for Worcester, Massachusetts, in the

summer of 1986. I had to sign a discharge form stating I was leaving the hospital against medical advice. When I was wheeled into the auditorium my heart sank. There were some four thousand people. There was a stage in the middle of the room, a man walking around, and people singing. I thought then, So, here is a man walking around waving his arms. Oh no, not another one of those revival meetings where people roll on the ground!

Well, I saw a nun who said she had been deaf until she was healed by God through Father DiOrio. Father spoke to her and she could hear him. Still, I was not convinced. Perhaps she was not really a nun. Perhaps she was pretending to be deaf. I found out later that she was a nun, and I no longer doubt her truthfulness.

You must realize that for fifteen years I was in research and depended on cold, hard facts alone. Proven facts, controlled facts, would convince me. Compared to me, the people who say "Show me" are very gullible people who will believe anything.

I arrived at the service with one percent belief and 99 percent disbelief. As I saw Father DiOrio walking toward me, and people being healed along his path, I said to God, "I know You perform miracles. I know You parted the Red Sea. I know that You helped me during the war. It is not You, Lord, that I am doubting. It is Father DiOrio. You have given me the intelligence that causes me to doubt. Lord, if I am wrong to disbelieve, forgive me and help me to believe."

So Father walked along blessing people, then he blessed me on the forehead. I felt a strange calm come upon me, then he went on blessing others until suddenly he turned and rushed back to me, put his face within five inches of mine, and said, "You have work yet to do." I thought to myself, I'm semiretired, with little work to do now and even less left to do, but I did not bother to question him. I just sat in my wheelchair, and he went on. When the meeting started to break up, the oxygen mask which I had been wearing with no problem for months started chafing and irritating my eyebrow. It hurt me, so I took it off. To my surprise, I could breathe easily. So, I told myself, just as a car in a garage uses little gasoline, a man sitting down does not need much oxygen. Why shouldn't I be able to breathe? But now that my face was exposed and everybody could see me, I felt ashamed that a big man like myself had to be wheeled out. So I told my attendants I wanted to try to walk at least to the incline. They could easily grab my elbows and shove me back into the wheelchair if I faltered. So I walked to the incline and felt fine. I walked up the incline. I felt fine. I walked to a level spot, then up about seven steps, and I felt fine. Seven steps! At home I would walk up one step and the second step would be like a knife driven into my heart. No matter how I demanded myself to walk, the pain would nail me to the spot. Now I walked with no effort, across level areas, then up more steps, and so on. I walked all the way to my car and said, "Look, I'm going to drive. You guys jump in back." I drove back here to Niantic, went out to dinner, popped a bottle of champagne, and celebrated. I am telling this story months later, and I no longer use any oxygen, pain medication, or heart medicine. I had become addicted to the morphine, so I went through terrible bone pain for three days while my body went through withdrawal.

The doctors at Peter Brent Brigham Hospital in Boston heard I was claiming this miracle, and asked me to submit to tests. I agreed to a thallium scan and stress tests. I endured the stress tests incredibly well, and the scan showed no dark areas in my heart. In fact, remarkably, my body had developed collaterals, which are methods of sending blood past the occluded areas. This simply cannot happen instantaneously. Because I was fine, I was released from the hospital after a few days. Since that time, I have been swimming in my swimming pool and dancing those strenuous American dances.

In conclusion, I want to say this. I had a heart disease which was absolutely fatal and incurable medically. Medically, what has happened to me is not possible. An artery which is blocked should have killed me. A miracle has happened to me. God has favored Father Ralph A. DiOrio by transmitting His miracle through him. I thank God and Father DiOrio for my life, and I will continue to use it to serve God.

PRAYER

Dear Lord, or should I say Divine Physician, I am just a simple man transformed by Your grace to a healed man. You are the One who truly heals the soul and, through Your message of salvation, delivers wholeness.

As I pray, dear Lord, Your holy word permeates my spirit, saying, "I am ready to hear . . . and to grant their requests. Let them but ask." Lord, in this contemporary age of materialism and scientific wonder, one almost becomes a stranger to the signs and wonders of God. I defend the phenomena of signs and wonders because I have been healed and know firsthand the wonders of the Lord. As a physician, I am trained to analyze absolute fact, to diagnose and determine prognosis. Day in and day out my educated mind and energies expend themselves. Truly, dear God, I have done my best in my professional vocation. I thank You for this gift of service.

One day, however, like a thief in the night, evil befell me. Like a Father Damien, apostle to the lepers, I became a victim of human illness. No longer did I deal with pain only through my patients. I felt it in my own body. Through my pain and suffering I came to know my need to touch You, the Divine Physician.

Lord, good comes out of evil. Your grace spoke to me through my illness. You introduced me to greater dimensions and obligations as part of my divine healing. As You laid Your wounded hands on me through Your authentic healing minister, Father DiOrio, You made me realize that Your eyes are watching all who live good lives. You listen and answer when they call You.

May all who read this story come to know that You listen to everyone who calls to You and You grant anything in line with Your will. In that spirit I received my healing. I thank You, Wounded Divine Physician and Healer.

"God's Compassion for His Child"

Sarah Pesto
Gainesville, Florida

Healing: Abnormal chloride level,
possible cystic fibrosis

Train up a child in the way he should go,
Even when he is old he will not depart from it.
(Proverbs 22:6)

A child has a thirst for learning and discovery that gives way to delight without skepticism. With their open minds and unswollen egos, children readily accept God's works and omnipotence. Susan Pesto's daughter, Sarah, opened her heart to Jesus and was healed, as Mrs. Pesto tells you here. But first let me share with you a beautiful, touching letter I received from Sarah, a truly memorable girl, in 1984. May she warm your heart as she warmed mine.

Dear Father DiOrio,

I enjoyed your healing service. I liked it when people were getting out of their wheel chairs and walking around the room. I liked to see that blind people were seeing things.

I am 9 years old. This past March I went to your healing service and was healed of my abnormal sweat test. I went to Shands Hospital in April. My sweat test was normal. My Mommy was thanking God and we all were happy.

I hope you have a Merry Christmas. I am a third grade student at St. Patrick's school in Gainesville.

Love,
Sarah Pesto

This testimony is in regard to the healing of our daughter, Sarah Pesto, who is now eleven years old[1]

---

[1] Sarah was eleven years old in 1986.

and in the fifth grade at St. Patrick's School, Gainesville, Florida.

Sarah had always been small for her age. During kindergarten she was sick with pneumonia, strep throat, and mononucleosis.

In the spring of 1983, her pediatrician decided to do a sweat test for cystic fibrosis, an incurable, often fatal disease involving the respiratory system, pancreas, and sweat glands. A sweat test measures the amount of chloride in the sweat. Normal ranges are up to 40 mEq/liter. Sarah's test, given at Shands Hospital, measured 64 mEq/liter. A repeat test carried out several days later was 58 mEq/liter. Her pediatrician said Sarah would need another test in the spring of 1984.

My husband and I decided to take Sarah to Father DiOrio's healing service here in Gainesville, Florida, on March 17, 1984. Her repeat sweat test was scheduled for April. During the beautiful service we prayed for our needs and for the needs of others. We were praying that Sarah's sweat test would show normal chloride levels. I remember even hoping that it would be half of what it was.

Near the end of the service Father anointed Sarah and she rested in the Holy Spirit. Throughout the service we could feel the gentle and loving presence of Jesus, and Sarah said she felt a sensation like soft feathers on her arms and legs.

Sarah went for the sweat test during Easter week that April. We were so happy when the doctor called with test results indicating a chloride level of 32 mEq/liter.

Since then, Sarah has grown six inches and is now four feet six inches tall. Although she is still slender, she loves swimming, playing her flute, and playing and running outdoors with her younger sister, Mary, and her younger brother, John.

My husband, John, and I thank and praise God the Father, the Son, and the Holy Spirit for answering our prayers.

PRAYER

Dear Jesus, I am only a child and so I have a child's mind and speak with a child's tongue.

I was ill, very ill, but Mom and Dad and friends said You cared. I am glad You care and I am glad You are God. What would we do without You!

The world, they say, is all mixed up. Maybe You will straighten it all out. I know You can. If You can heal me, and if You are God, You certainly will allow people to use their hearts, minds, and goodwill to do the right things.

I'm so glad You loved me in this special way of healing me. I used to feel so sad. So many times when I was sick I felt different from my classmates and friends. It is such a humiliating thing to feel different from everyone, but then You know that because You, too, were different.

You know something, dear Lord: I really believe You healed me fully. I believe this because You are no stranger to suffering. You suffered so much. Thank You, dear Jesus. You're my champ! You're the best!

Oh, before I close my prayer, please remember to continue blessing my dad, mom, sister Mary, and brother Johnny. Bless all the world. Oh, and please keep blessing Father Ralph, too. Thank You!

"Please, God, Give Us a Baby"

Jeanne P. Dolan
Newport, Rhode Island

Healing: Infertility

Of every child who is born, under no matter what circumstances, and of no matter what parents, the potentiality of the human race is born again; and in him, too, once more, and of each of us, our terrific responsibility towards human life; towards the utmost idea of goodness, and of the horror of error, and of God. (James Agee)

Medically, the definition of infertility is the inability to cause pregnancy within a specified period of time, usually a year. Emotionally, the diagnosis is devastating to the man and woman who planned to build their lives around their child. The woman dreams of feeling her baby move within her. Together she and her husband watch parents in supermarkets and on beaches playing with their children, cuddling them, leading them. "Why not us?" childless parents ask themselves as they stare in silence, smiling weakly.

Next to salvation, a child is God's greatest gift to us. Through the miracle of His love, he allows the love between a husband and a wife to create a new life. At first the tiny baby depends entirely on mother for life. Then, ever so gradually, God prepares the child for independence. The helpless newborn weans from mother, walks toward—then away from—father, and leaves the parents' home for his own. The gift requires so much from those to whom it is entrusted. The work and worry seem endless at times, yet actually last for only a moment. It is that moment that the Dolans craved.

For most couples, bringing together a sperm and egg to develop into a baby is taken for granted. For couples diagnosed as infertile, conceiving can become a consuming struggle. The hows and whens of conception, trips to fertility specialists, and well-meaning advice from friends fill their days and their minds. While the medical profession has helped many, only God can remove any and all obstacles. Only God can give a child, as Jeanne and Jim Dolan know. Jeanne explains.

Life is so very precious. I'm speaking about human life, the life of individual people. Christ tells us,

"I have come that men may have life and may have it in all its fullness." (John 10:10)

God, the Lord of life, has given men and women the ministry of safeguarding life. From the moment of its conception, life is to be guarded with the greatest of care.

To respect and foster human life is to glorify and honor God, the Creator of all persons. Each of us is to realize the value of our own lives as well as the lives of others.

Until recently I didn't reflect much on the sanctity of life. We usually don't think much about such matters until something causes us to do so. My reason was simple. My husband, Jim, and I had desperately wanted to have children but had none.

It all began in the spring of 1978, when I started taking oral contraceptives. I wanted to get used to them before our wedding took place in October. The following May I went off the pill and for nine months did not have a menstrual flow. Jim and I were examined by a local gynecologist at that time. When my husband was found to be fine, an oral fertility medication was prescribed for me along with a hormone to initiate my menstrual flow. Thereafter, I scheduled relations with Jim. Despite increasing doses of medication, this monthly cycle of events continued for eighteen months without conception taking place.

In January 1982 we decided to seek the advice of a specialist in Boston, who scheduled me for exploratory surgery in April. My fallopian tubes were found to be clear, but my doctor discovered polycystic ovarian disease. I was told that this disease could be the result of having taken an excessive amount of the prescribed oral fertility medicine. We were invited to take part in a study to test an isolated hormone that I was lacking in my cycle. This particular hormone, FSH (follicle-stimulating hormone), helps to produce the egg at the beginning of the cycle. Following some discussion with our family, we decided to give it a try.

So for the next two and a half weeks, until the time for ovulation when the egg would be released, I received daily intramuscular injections that Jim was taught to give me. Although it must have been difficult for him to do this, he never complained. Meanwhile, I also had frequent blood tests and took numerous eight-hour bus trips to Boston so that my progress and egg growth could be monitored by ultrasound. Then, as ovulation approached, Jim and I had to have more frequent relations on demand. The stress grew to be unbearable! We were still unsuccessful. Having reached my limit, I wrote to the doctor and told him that we had decided to apply for adoption. It was in that May of 1982 that we, in fact, did apply to adopt an infant, completing the initial papers in August. By then I was just beginning to unwind from all of the medical treatment and stress.

Through the grace of God and goodness of friends, we were fortunate to attend a noon Mass said by Father Ralph A. DiOrio on September 1, 1982, in the Apostolate of Prayer chapel in Leicester, Massachusetts. After it was over, Father DiOrio prayed over my husband and me. I rested in the Spirit for a while, feeling very peaceful.

The Lord did not delay. In exactly one week I received my first miracle! I actually started my first menstrual flow, without drugs, since before I had gone on the pill way back in May of 1978. I had subsequent normal monthly flows until April. On May 20, 1983, I was told of our great miracle! I was pregnant! The doctor determined that I was in my first month. God was blessing our marriage with a child! Yes, He was actually making it possible for us to cooperate with Him in the making of human life.

Eight months passed, and finally, at three o'clock

in the morning of January 3, 1984, I was admitted to the hospital. Jim stayed with me throughout my seven-hour labor and at 10:14 A.M. Thomas Joseph Dolan came into this world. He weighed six pounds fifteen and a half ounces and had the most beautiful blue eyes. His hair was brown, like ours, and he was twenty and three-quarters inches long. We were simply ecstatic! How true are the words of St. John, "When a woman . . . is delivered of the child, she no longer remembers the anguish, for joy that a child is born into the world." (John 16:21)

A few days later we brought our precious baby home, and on the feast of St. Thomas Aquinas (January 28, 1984) he was baptized "Thomas Joseph," after both of his grandfathers.

Tommy is now three years old and has been blessed with good health and a cheerful disposition, and each time I see his smile I'm reminded of how special he is. In July of 1985 God blessed all of us with a baby girl, Mary Elizabeth. Each time I see them smile I am reminded of how special they are. Since He blessed me with His gift of new life I've spent an hour each day in prayer. During that time, while my babies are sleeping, I often draw close to Mary and whisper to her:

> "My soul magnifies the Lord
>   and my spirit rejoices in God my Savior
> For He has looked upon His servant
>   in her lowliness . . .
> God who is mighty
>   has done great things for me!"

The Dolans' physician wrote to Father DiOrio regarding Mrs. Dolan after she became pregnant with Tommy. Here is what he had to say: "She has a long-

standing history of infertility secondary to anovulation (not producing eggs) which has been resistant to all available treatment for ovulation induction. We have been pleasantly surprised to learn that she became pregnant sometime in [the] winter of 1983 and her expected date of confinement is mid–late December, 1983."

PRAYER

Dear Lord, I was shocked and frightened when I thought I might never bear a life within the willing tabernacle of my human body.

Continuous failure to conceive distressed me and filled me with anxiety. From the depths of my total womanhood I remembered You, my God, my Life, my Source, my Strength. O Lord, how true it is that we go as far as our prayer. My prayer was one of need, but it also had its noble reason. I am a woman; I am a bride, but I wanted a child with my wonderful husband. We both wanted a trinity of love. We wanted a home!

O God, God, God! You are always so ready to hear! So ready to minister to us who would accept the beauty and nobility of that precious grace— motherhood!

How can I thank You, dear heavenly Father, for blessing me with fruition. I am not sterile! I am Your divine creation, a creative potential for life far beyond the biological.

This whole prayer, Lord, is one of adoration for You because it is founded on all-embracing gratitude. Gratitude for what? Gratitude for al- lowing my whole womanhood to realize and accept its singular beauty; that my dear husband whom I love so much would have the infinite joy of holding our little child. It just seems so right, dear Lord, that husband and children go hand in hand because they are so important, perhaps even more important than they realize.

I thank You, dear Father, for allowing me to feel like a whole woman in spirit, soul, and body. All of me, Lord, desperately yearns for the fulfillment of my womanhood to be affirmed by You and my husband. I am pleased to be what I am, a woman fully capable of working hand in hand with You, my God, to bring forth another human life. Oh how I longed for conception, that first moment when life was created in my womb. Yes, by Your providential hand I was able to conceive and bear a child. You made me worthy of Your creation and of experiencing a child's affection and trust.

Thank You, Lord, for making our house not just a place with four walls, but a home where father, mother, and child live in faith, hope, and love!

"Don't Let My Boy Die"

Eric Hanson
Hawthorn Woods, Illinois

Healing: Ependymomas

Once when some mothers were bringing their children to Jesus to bless them, the disciples shooed them away, telling them not to bother him.

But when Jesus saw what was happening he was very much displeased with his disciples and said to them, "Let the children come to me, for the Kingdom of God belongs to such as they. Don't send them away!" (Mark 10:13–14)

A child is a precious gift from God, one that we parents assume we will have forever. We plan our child's future. Shall he play soccer or softball; learn a trade or attend college? His successes are our successes. His failure is our failure.

We feel his pain. We wrap our lives around him. What could be more heart wrenching than to watch our own child writhe in pain, then be told death will take him from us? That is what happened to little Eric Hanson and his parents when Eric was just five years old. Eric was diagnosed as having malignant ependymomas, a tumor in the membrane lining of a ventricle in the brain. Devastated, the Hansons trudged through each day of Eric's illness, plodding against a wave of grief and helplessness, until they brought their precious son to Father Ralph A. DiOrio and asked God, the Divine Healer, to save their child. Just as Jesus felt compassion for the sick and healed them when He walked the earth, He feels compassion now and heals. Eric's mother, Paulette Hanson, never will forget Eric's journey through agony and back. Her life, as well as Eric's, has been changed. She walks more closely with Jesus now, and through Him knows a special peace only He can grant.

Our nightmare began in December of 1979. My husband, Philip, my son, Eric, and my daughter, Jennie, and I were headed to my parents' home in northern New York to make funeral arrangements for my husband's grandfather. It was that weekend that our five-year-old son, Eric, started getting sick. He had vomited several times over the weekend, but we attributed it to the fact that the weekend had been highly emotionally charged. We assumed Eric had been upset by it all. He continued vomiting once a week through Christmas. We brought him to the doctor for blood work and checkups, and our pediatrician told us Eric probably had a virus of unknown origin.

We watched Eric grow weaker each day. It got to be a routine at our house, Eric's illness. He got up every morning, went to the bathroom, and vomited clear fluid. Then he lay down on the cold tile with his face on the floor and stayed there for a while. He used to say, "It feels so good, Mom, the cold floor. I'll be all right in a minute." This is how he was until after the New Year.

Eric began having headaches. On the way to school one morning he stumbled, picked himself up, sat down on his lunch box, and vomited. I called the doctor and Eric was admitted to the hospital that morning. After a barrage of tests, I received the unbelievable news, a brain tumor. "Your son will have a shunt put in to relieve pressure on the brain. Then he will have more surgery to try to remove the tumor. Most likely the tumor will be malignant and he might receive radiation and chemotherapy after he regains his strength."

I remember putting down the telephone. The silence in the room was maddening. We were so alone and frightened. The words kept ringing through my mind—brain tumor. How could this be happening to us?

The news was earth shattering to everyone. It's hard to describe my feelings at the time. I guess a part of me was in mourning already. I couldn't eat, think, or talk to anyone. I kept thinking that this was all part of a very bad dream and I would wake up. Somehow it would all be over.

The surgery was scheduled within a few days. It all seemed so unnatural. Just having to look at him all curled up in that hospital bed, watch those brown pained eyes, and hide our concern for him was more than my husband and I could bear. It was the most difficult time of our lives.

Eric got through the seven-hour surgery very well. Each minute that passed seemed an eternity. I prayed for a miracle, that the tumor would be totally removed, but it didn't happen that way. It was 8:30 P.M. when the neurosurgeon sat down with us in the hospital lobby. We had been waiting since 9:15 A.M. and we were mentally and physically exhausted. It was like a judge passing sentence. "We got 95 percent of the tumor. It was malignant. You'll probably have two years, possibly five to seven with him, if you're lucky. Time will be precious."

How I had hated that minute and those words. Where was the God who had helped me before? Why had he let this happen to us! I felt empty, sick, and bitter. I had all I could do to face my son in the intensive care unit at 11:30 P.M. Eric was so ashen. He was swollen and very still. Tubes and signs were planted all over his head telling the nurses where not to touch or move him. He was hooked up to intravenous bottles and equipment. My husband and I just clung to the sides of his bed and gazed. It was all so hopeless. I turned from his bed and ran down the hall with tears streaming down my face. My husband followed. The silence was deadening. I continued to pray silently for God's help.

Eric stayed in intensive care for a week. Then he was transferred to the pediatric unit for four weeks. I can't begin to describe the torment I experienced as I watched my son go through hell. No one ever can imagine the suffering children go through with such an illness. He had withered from fifty pounds down to twenty-nine. He had become almost unrecognizable. Our son was always curled in the fetal position clinging to his bedrail when I went in for our daily routine. He got so he wouldn't function without his dad or me around him all the time. A string of doctors strolled in and out of his room. His case was so rare that every new doctor would probe and pick at him until he screamed at the sight of anyone in white.

Blood tests got to be like torture. They had tapped him so many times that his veins had collapsed. It took four people to hold him down in the treatment room as they drew fluid from his neck to relieve the pressure on his brain. He screamed endlessly as I just stood outside in the corridor and cried with him, praying that God would get him through just one more time.

Here is where I must interrupt my story because this is when our Lord started directing me. One day my mom called me. She was very excited and hopeful. She had come upon a *Catholic Digest* in the bathroom closet. We had never subscribed to it, but my dad, being a rural carrier, and Catholic, had it in the backseat of his car. Somehow it found its way into our home. The words on the cover, "Does faith healing really work," stood out dramatically and caught my mom's eye. [Note: Father DiOrio is not a faith healer. He is an instrument through which God heals.] She and Dad read it and were so excited about it that they decided to send it to us.

My husband and I were in awe after reading it. We decided to go to Worcester, Massachusetts, to see this incredible man, Father Ralph A. DiOrio, and see if he could really help us as he had helped so many others. We planned to go in a few months during our vacation. Within a few days of reading the article, I went to my son's radiation treatment early and happened to meet a young woman and her son who were running late for his treatment. Her little boy had leukemia. As she and I sat talking about our faith, she said, "My prayers have been answered! Father DiOrio is coming to my parish!" Funny thing, I had never heard of this man until a few days ago and had never met this woman until today. Little did I know that God was setting me up!

I went with my friend to see Father DiOrio on Saint Patrick's Day in 1980 and it was on that night, while holding my son in my arms, that our Lord left a sign that everything was going to be all right. Father DiOrio was praying over a woman who had a brain tumor. While he prayed he said that there were others there who had brain tumors, possibly a child, who would be healed. I felt sick inside as I heard the words. How could all this be happening? Why was I sent here? My friend tried to push me up to have this wonderful man touch my son. I could not move. My stomach was on fire. I just held my sleeping child in my arms and prayed.

I saw miracles that night and went away with faith stronger than I had ever known. Somehow I knew that this message was for me and that God had arranged all of this. It was all such a neat package, perhaps a bit unbelievable to some of you reading this, but then God always did the unbelievable, didn't He!

After all of this happened, Eric continued to have radiation treatments to the head and spine. We were forced to stop halfway through the treatments because Eric's blood counts became critically low. Our doctor suggested that we take him to Children's Hospital for a second opinion. We went from bad news to worse. The size and location of the tumor made eliminating it impossible regardless of the treatment. He said the tumor was high grade, that is, very malignant, so we would be lucky to have six months with Eric. The doctor said he would not bother with chemotherapy, and suggested we try to let Eric enjoy the last few months drug-free.

I drove home really down that day but soon remembered the service with Father DiOrio. I was more determined to fight and pray and prove all those doctors wrong. I delighted in the fact that God said He would help us, and I was going to show the world that we could get through this with His help.

After Eric finished going to radiation treatments and underwent chemotherapy, his doctor ordered a CAT scan that came back negative, meaning that there was no sign of the tumor. He cautioned us, however, that there could be malignant cells floating around in other areas of the brain, but I knew right then what had happened. It was all so overwhelming to me, but I believe a healing took place that night with Father DiOrio. Eric finished chemotherapy years ago and has been an inspiration to the doctors, nurses, and patients.

We've spread our great news everywhere and we thank everyone who has prayed for Eric. Even people who did not know Eric prayed for him. It was all of you who made this possible. You all talked to God and he listened to you and watched over us during those difficult moments. Jesus is not dead. He is very much alive. He very cleverly turned my nonbelief into belief. These events didn't just happen by themselves.

AUTHOR'S NOTE:

Eric, twelve years old when this report was written, is testimony of God's healing powers and love. Medical records written before Eric saw Father DiOrio, state his prognosis as "dreadful," with a 20 percent chance of living until he was seven years old. As of May 1986, Eric's physician estimated Eric's chance of long-term survival at 80 to 85 percent because the type tumor he was treated for sometimes recurs after ten to twenty years. The prognosis: optimistic. Periodic checkups are required.

PRAYER

Dear God, You are always in search of us. You seem to come to us in quiet steps and apparently slip away after bestowing signs and wonders. What a magnificent God You are! I came to know Your magnificence when You blessed and healed my son. You seem to thrive on loving us, by giving us visible proof of just how loving You are.

My prayer is simply, Thank You, dear Lord, not only for touching my son's brain tumor, but also for touching me and my family. Your divine healing hand is so comprehensive that in one sweep you rallied us all.

What can I do to show my gratitude? I can only praise You and glorify You. I only can live the rest of my life for You, bearing in mind Your concern for others.

In gratitude, I will never be afraid to tell the world that the God of Creation never gives up on us, never lets us go without a benediction. Oh, if only we humans would take the time to reflect on priorities—our souls, our eternal destiny. How true it is that there is even hope for a tree that has been cut down. It sprouts again and grows tender, new branches.

Already I see the result of my son's healing; a quiet growth in grace and character. Thank You, dear Jesus, for Your constant goodness.

"He's Healing Me, Mom"

Jeanine Marson
Cranford, New Jersey

Healing: Scoliosis

"But the good soil represents the hearts of those who truly accept God's message and produce a plentiful harvest for God—thirty, sixty, or even a hundred times as much as was planted in their hearts." Then He asked them, "When someone lights a lamp, does he put a box over it to shut out the light? Of course not! The light couldn't be seen or used. A lamp is placed on a stand to shine and be useful." (Mark 4:20–21)

For those unfamiliar with God's true powers, it may be inconceivable that He could actually reach out and straighten a crooked spine. Perhaps that is one of the reasons God chose this young woman's spinal column for His miracle. The S curve of Jeanine Marson's spine had been well documented by doctors, and Jeanine has sent us her doctor's report attesting to the fact that her spine now is straight. For those who need to see it to believe it, a photograph showing Jeanine's newly straightened spine tells it all.

Jeanine Marson, nineteen, has had juvenile rheumatoid arthritis since 1974 and had developed a scoliosis of her spine in the area between her neck and her abdomen. Instead of holding Jeanine upright, her spine leaned her upper body to the left, causing her pain. Here is her story.

In August of 1985, my mother and I went on a pilgrimage led by Father Ralph A. DiOrio to the Shrine of Lourdes in France. On our return flight, Father was stopping by each row of seats blessing everyone and silently praying for a moment. When he came to our seats he did the same thing. I was watching him. When he finished praying he looked at me, then placed his hand on top of my head, closed his eyes, and briefly prayed. Then he made the sign of the cross and continued on his way.

While he had his hand on my head, I felt a cool breeze go through me. A few minutes later my back started to ache, so I asked for some pillows so I could get comfortable. By the time I got home, the pain in my entire spine was intense. My mother was dismayed that I was feeling worse, because we had just been to the baths at Lourdes and through the entire spiritual experience. I went straight to bed. The following day my mother asked me how I felt. I told her that my spine was still painful. Again she expressed dismay and said, "But I took you to Lourdes to get well!" I told her sometimes you get worse before you get better and maybe I actually was being healed. She said, "That's right." The next day when I awakened I had no more pain and I felt fine.

About three weeks later, as my mother was helping me wash my back, she discovered that my scoliosis was completely gone. My spine, after six years of being scoliotic, was now straight and healed.

PRAYER

Lord Jesus, sometimes I not only wonder but marvel at how You keep us simple and teachable, even when we forget our dependence on You. Life has a way, with all its circumstances, to make us see how little we are without You.

Lord, sometimes I wonder if You are not laughing at us, at our ways of searching for the best. Our ways are so humanly oriented while Yours are so divine. The difference between our human way and Your divine route is that Your plan incorporates the abundant fullness of our every need.

You healed me, Lord! And from the depths of my human spirit I raise up my sentiment of gratitude. When You healed me in that airplane en route from Lourdes to New York, I was almost like a desperate soul hanging on in spite of doubt. It probably could be identified as the eleventh hour—a twilight of possible frenzy!

O, how different are Your ways. My mother and I prayed zealously, humanly, for a stunning miracle shot at Lourdes. Oh we humans, how spectacular are our aspirations! I was so engrossed in my mother's desire and my own longings, that I did not realize my pilgrimage to Lourdes was simply a stepping-stone to revive my discouraged spirit.

Lord, at that grace-filled grotto of Marsabielle, were You actually summoning me to first rededicate my soul to You? And then, after I wholeheartedly beheld Your face in righteousness, You satisfied my need for healing. Oh, I shall never forget that moment when I awoke in the quiet of my room to behold Your healing touch.

"By His Grace"

Sister Urban Geoffroy, D.H.S.
Daughters of the Holy Spirit
Chicopee, Massachusetts

*Healing: Shortness of breath
and wheezing*

"So don't be anxious about tomorrow. God will take care of your tomorrow too. Live one day at a time."
(Matthew 6:34)

Sister Urban Geoffroy is an active eighty-eight-year-old nun who received an unexpected healing. She had readily accepted her physical problems but, nevertheless, a loving God bestowed the gift of good health upon her. Sister Geoffroy's physician, Raymond L. Gagnon, M.D., is excited about his patient's miracle, and joyfully welcomes God as a partner in his medical practice.

In a letter to me, Dr. Gagnon explained that Sister Geoffroy's health problems had been slowing her down for several months in early 1986. He writes, "I was seeing her every three months for mild hypertension, arteriosclerotic heart disease (characterized by thickening and hardening of the arteries), and mild clinical congestive heart failure, for which she was taking a diuretic and [other] medications.

"When I saw her on April 25, 1986, she was complaining of pain . . . and mostly of increased shortness of breath when climbing stairs, and wheezing even on level ground. She was anxious, upset, afraid of not being able to continue her ministry, consisting of visiting the sick and bringing Jesus to them."

Dr. Gagnon said he gave Sister Geoffroy a prescription for digitalis (a heart stimulant), and for increased diuretics. As it turned out, he reports, Sister Geoffroy did not have the prescriptions filled before she was healed. Dr. Gagnon writes: "This does not surprise me, for He is always there to reveal to me how much [God the] Father loves us. I hope Jesus will guide me about her prescriptions during the next visits. Yes, Jesus is alive. He is the King, Savior, Healer."

And now Sister Geoffroy tells her story.

For several months I had been coughing, a dry cough, and wheezing. I was also short of breath when

I climbed stairs and walked up hills. I thought it was just old age creeping up. After all, I was born in 1898.

I ended up going to see the doctor, who prescribed cough syrup and other medicines. I visited the doctor during the next few months and took my medication as advised. On April 25, 1986, the doctor prescribed a heart medicine that I was to start taking April 28.

On April 27, I attended one of Father DiOrio's healing services in Worcester, Massachusetts, with the intention of praying for my niece, who has terminal cancer. I was unable to meet with Father DiOrio personally that day, but still hoped something would happen. Father had said that some people would be healed during the service, others would be healed on their way home, and still more would improve after reaching home.

We were on our way home when suddenly I realized I wasn't wheezing anymore. I felt as though I was breathing much better, in fact, normally. I said to those in the van, "I am healed." We all thanked God and praised Him. I have not been bothered with wheezing since the healing.

Dr. Gagnon gives witness to this healing. I am still active, although I turned eighty-eight years old July 4, 1986. I was a teacher for over fifty years, then I was a tutor in our school to help children who need to improve their work. Since 1976 I have been working as a member of the Retired Senior Volunteer Program in the Adult Health Center here in Chicopee. As a commissioned extraordinary minister of the Eucharist, I bring Holy Communion to the elderly and sick who are unable to come to Mass.

I thank God that He has given me good health and keeps me in His care.

PRAYER

*As a religious woman, I am invited by You to
serve unconditionally. How easy it was way back
then to proclaim my religious vows. I was at a
tender age, untouched by life's promises and inex-
perienced in life's conditions.*

*As time unfolded, however, I matured into
religious union with You and immersed myself in
Your message:* **The way of love is the way to live.**

*In the twilight of my life, dear Lord, You fill
every nook and cranny of my being. I spent my
years ardently and fully as I professed. Poverty
had its deprivations; chastity had its one love, You.
Obedience provided liberation, and although pain
had a role in my life, it never squeezed out the joy.*

*One pain nearly wiped me out, dear Lord, but
You unexpectedly healed me. I'll never forget that
day. I did not seek Your healing love for myself,
but for someone else. Why do You love me so
much? All I need is Your love. It is my love for You
that called me to Your service.*

*When You, Lord, receive our sincere prayers,
You allow us to give glory to God by uniting our
sacrifice with Yours. When You hear us pray so
sincerely, You carry out our prayers by inviting us
to the mystery of redemptive pain.*

*Pain is so real! Few accept it. An authentic
Christian, a dedicated, religious servant, knows
better. Such is the lot of earthly mortals who aspire
to sanctity. This is the crown of eternal glory for
those who dare to walk with You, dear Lord. These
Calvary steps not only lead to Crucifixion, but also*

follow the steps of those who go to the tomb to find You, their resurrected Lord.

I guess You spared me to continue working for You. There is much to do. I must continue sharing my story, interceding for others, loving others, and touching human lives.

"Remember Me, God?"

Barbara MacRae
Marshfield, Massachusetts

Healing: Cancer

I shall not die but live: and declare the works of the Lord. (From The Book of Common Prayer, lb. 17)

Cancer. Although doctors and researchers have made great strides in recent years, curing more and more cancers, the word still conjures images of pale, drawn faces and withered, pained bodies. Fear and death come quickly to mind. Frequent breast checks save many but breast cancer still kills 40,200 people a year, including 300 men, according to the American Cancer Society's 1986 statistics. It strikes one in eleven women, mostly over age thirty-five, and is a major cause of death in women ages forty to forty-four, the American Cancer Society tells us. Father DiOrio stresses the importance of regular visits to your doctor and strongly urges you to insist that your medical concerns be adequately investigated. In short, take responsibility for your well-being. Barbara MacRae's attempts for early detection were blocked, but Jesus scooped her up in his arms and took care of her.

My doctor made a mistake. He thought I had a cyst. When I went for my yearly checkup in the fall of 1977 and expressed concern about a lump in my left breast, he told me to watch it and call him if it became a problem. It did become a problem and he instructed me to put hot compresses on it, but they didn't help. When I called my doctor a third time he was annoyed. He let me know that he was fed up with all of the silly little complaints that he heard from "his girls" and told me to try cold compresses. When they were not effective, I decided to ignore my condition.

By New Year's Day, 1978, I was tired most of the time and quite uncomfortable. However, I did find a comfortable position in which to hold my head. I also held my left arm up with my right one because if I didn't, it hurt. In short, I learned to live with it. In early May I had an appointment with my orthodontist and drove to his office using one arm. He noticed that I had difficulty getting into the chair and suggested that I call upstairs for an appointment with my doctor. I said that I didn't want to bother the doctor with my small problems because I wasn't due for a checkup until fall. The orthodontist called my doctor, who then scheduled me for a mammogram on Tuesday. He planned to drain the cyst the next day.

While the mammogram was being done, I heard a lot of commotion. When it was over, the technician asked for further X rays. Then, with genuine concern in his voice, he asked, "Mrs. MacRae, why did you let this go for so long?"

Late that afternoon I was sent to another hospital where I spent the next two days undergoing tests and answering questions from several physicians. The result of all the tests was that on May 11, our twentieth wedding anniversary, my husband and I were informed that I urgently needed a mastectomy. I was scheduled for surgery the next morning. I didn't say much. In fact, I don't even remember what I thought, although I do recall being wheeled into the operating room. The next thing I remember was someone saying I had to wake up because a handsome young man was waiting for me. It was my son, Randy, and I didn't want to miss seeing him. Suddenly I noticed something. My left breast was still there! For the next couple of days, I was packed in ice and people were unusually quiet while they visited me. Something was wrong and I knew it.

One afternoon not long after my operation, one of the doctors, a cancer specialist, came to my room. He stood looking out the window, his back to me. Finally I asked, "Well, what is it? Please tell me." Although he said he preferred to wait for my husband, I insisted he tell me immediately. Reluctantly he told me I was going to die. "Yes, I know. Everybody dies," I replied. Still looking out the window, he added, "If you're lucky you might live for three months." With that, my husband arrived and they went out of the room together, beyond my range of hearing.

Alone with my thoughts, I could not think clearly. Someone had been condemned to die. This time that someone was me. I thought of my poor husband who had just lost his mother, and I thought of our children. I did not want them to become orphans as I had. Then I said, "Hey, God, remember me from way back when? Please heal me. I'd like to see a grandchild or two." Having said what was on my mind, I fell asleep.

The following day I learned of the diagnosis. I had inflammatory cancer of the left breast that had spread to my lymph nodes and thoracic (upper body) spine. My doctor thought chemotherapy might slow the rapid progression of my illness. Believing that it was worth a try, I went for my first treatment on May 19. It was dreadful. Another treatment was scheduled. Seeing how intensely I was suffering, my husband contacted a friend who made a June 1 appointment for me at a Boston hospital. After completing tests, the doctors arrived at the same conclusion. There was no escaping it. I was going to die. But then the doctors told me of a test group that would start treatment soon. The forty-nine people who would take part all were in the last stages of cancer. The idea was to bombard the cancer with heavy doses of drugs in hopes of killing the cancer cells. What did I have to lose? So I signed my name on the dotted line, becoming the fiftieth person.

The treatment program was not easily tolerated, and I was to be on it for either eighteen months or until death do us part. By this time I had lost almost all my hair and my eyelashes were gone. My blood count fell drastically, making me extremely weak, and my body was thin and racked with pain. I felt I was a tremendous burden on my family and could see only darkness ahead. It was during one of these dark moments that I remembered a passage I had once read in the Bible. It was this promise: "I am the light of the world. He who follows me will not walk in darkness, but will have the true light of life." (John 8:12)

We had planned to visit friends but I felt too exhausted to make the trip. When my husband called to explain, our friends insisted that we come to their home. So we went off to Leominster, Massachusetts. After we got settled, they asked if we had ever heard of Father DiOrio. Although we did not know of him, I was willing to try anything. It just so happened that Father DiOrio was having a service that night in St. John's Church in Worcester.

On July 6, 1978, we arrived at the church three hours before the service was to begin. Already the entire area was jammed with people. It was very hot, yet no one made a move to leave. I found myself worrying about others who were there, although looking back I doubt that many were more seriously ill than I was.

Three hours after the service began, Father DiOrio said he was going to minister to the sick as the Holy Spirit moved him to do so. Immediately he called out, "There is a woman here who is being healed of breast cancer and she is dressed in black and white. Would she please stand up!" Because I was wearing blue and white I thought that it couldn't be me. But Father persistently called for the same person until finally he said, "Would every woman with breast cancer please stand up." About fifty women rose from their seats, including me. Father looked around and suddenly pointed at me, saying, "It's you, honey! Come around here." "Oh, Jesus can do anything," I said. "Do you believe in the power of the Holy Spirit?" he asked. When I answered yes, Father told me to close my eyes and thank Jesus. I did and the next thing that I was aware of was a feeling of deep contentment within me as I seemed to rush toward a beautiful light. Someone I could not see said, "You have to go back," and repeated, "You have to go back." I don't want to go back, I thought, and woke up lying on the floor of the church. Then I heard Father's gentle voice as he asked me, "What are you doing down there?" I quickly answered that I didn't know and he told me to get up. With my back straight I rose from the floor with remarkable ease. The tumor was gone! I was so stunned that I was unable to speak, except to say thank you. By this time my husband was with me and I could hear sounds of clapping throughout the church. But more than anything else I was aware that all pain had left me and I was walking with my back straight once again.

When we arrived home our neighbors could see that my condition had improved vastly. Our children were all excited and eager for me to return to the doctors to show them that I was cured. I went for a checkup on July 19 and the doctors couldn't find any trace of cancer. They ordered X rays and a bone scan and these showed no evidence of the disease. But the doctors seemed to think that perhaps the drugs had arrested my illness temporarily, so they strongly insisted that I remain in the experimental program that I had undertaken.

Needless to say, I was very upset until I called Father DiOrio's office to ask for advice. I was told to remain on medication until my doctors indicated otherwise and if God wanted me out of therapy, He would find a way.

So I obediently went to the hospital for my dosage of drugs along with the forty-nine other patients.

Although we did not all go at the same time, we often got to see each other. After a while I noticed that I wasn't seeing as many of them as I had seen originally. When I asked I was told that several of the patients had changed their days of treatment. I accepted this answer for a while, but when it reached the point that I saw the same few people all of the time, I figured out what had happened. It was two whole years after I had terminated therapy when a doctor told me that I was the only person from the entire test group who was alive!

Today I have two beautiful grandchildren. The little girl's name is Holly Miranda and she is named after our beloved son, Randy, who went to live with the Lord a year after I was healed. Our grandson's name is Matthew, meaning "gift from God." Often as I look at these two lovely children I become tearfully aware of how very good God is to grant my desire.

My life has changed dramatically. God gave me the gift of a new life on July 6, 1978. The way that I see it, every moment of my life now belongs to Him. As a Eucharistic minister, I enjoy the special privilege of bringing Communion to the sick in our hometown. How can I help but be reminded of God's great love for me? With deep appreciation, I seek to live every moment of my life to the fullest, in His name, so help me God!

PRAYER

Every morning I will joyfully thank the Lord for His kindness. Every evening as I tumble into a welcoming bed of rest, I will rejoice in the Lord's faithfulness. The Lord touched me, and He alone healed me of my anguish. In Him alone did I trust and He alone saved me. He saved me to trust in

Him for each day's problems. He saved me to live in vital union with Him. He saved me to convince me that when my roots are grown deep down in Him, I could go forth and teach every person I meet that they too can draw up nourishment from Him. Perhaps my healing of cancer was nothing more than a public witness of what Paul admonishes in Colossians 2:7, "See that you go on growing in the Lord and become strong and vigorous in the truth you were taught. Let your lives overflow with joy and thanksgiving for all He has done."

Prayer is always upon my lips, dear Lord, my prayer of gratitude. Now that I am healed I retrace the anguish that horrible, evil cancer caused in my life and I proclaim the praises of You, Lord, as I thank You.

I cannot help but conclude that God's healing is a result of His hunger to touch mankind with His love. In whatever time I have left, it shall be my just duty, my single-hearted love, to tell every human being how well God understands the evil one's harassment against all humanity. Forever I will herald that God will do something about the evil one's onslaughts. Lord, help me teach others what You taught me through Your healing love, that You, God, will emancipate us from the slavery of sin, sickness, and disease.

How true it is, Lord, that every circumstance in life has a teachable message. What have I learned? What can I proclaim to others who have become victims of Satan's harassment? Help me influence others with Your abiding words, "Be strong! Be courageous! Do not be afraid! For the Lord your God will be with you. He will neither fail you nor forsake you." (Deuteronomy 31:6)

"Go Tell It on the Mountain"

William E. O'Brien
Watervliet, New York

Healing: Rheumatoid arthritis

Marriage: It is the union of two souls in a strong love for the abolishment of separateness. It is that higher unity which fuses the separate unities within two spirits. It is the golden ring in a chain whose beginning is a glance, and whose end is Eternity. It is the pure rain that falls from an unblemished sky to fructify and bless the fields of divine Nature. (Kahlil Gibran)

In a strong marriage, the husband and wife feel each other's pain. When one is wounded the other cries, and when one is healed, both are joyfully relieved and thankful. William O'Brien sustained many injuries in an accident. His recovery was complicated by rheumatoid arthritis: a cruel, destructive disease that turns the body against itself. In its most serious form, rheumatoid arthritis causes painful, badly damaged joints. As the Arthritis Foundation explains, the immune system of people with this chronic disease seems to work incorrectly. The disease not only attacks the joints, but also can damage lungs, muscles, and blood vessels. There is no cure, but present treatments sometimes lessen some or all of the symptoms.

Here is Marion and William O'Brien's testimony of their pain and healing. William speaks first.

On December 28, 1975, while chopping ice off my roof, the ladder I was standing on slipped, dropping me thirty feet onto a blacktop driveway. I sustained fourteen fractures in the right side of my body, including a broken thigh bone. In addition, my knee was shattered. I had a concussion, a broken nose, and the inside of my mouth was torn to shreds.

Prior to the accident, I had suffered with rheumatoid arthritis for fifteen years. Now that so many bones were broken, I suffered in agony twenty-four hours a day. It was a miracle that I survived the fall, but I required eighty-one days of treatment in St. Mary's Hospital in Troy, New York. After returning home to continue my convalescence, I felt very fortunate to receive Channel 27 out of Worcester, Massachusetts, because that station carried a program featuring Father

Ralph A. DiOrio. I watched Father DiOrio many times and prayed that someday I would see him in person. In fact, I prayed for more than a year that I would someday receive his blessing.

On February 24, 1980, my so-called "good leg" gave out and I fell over. I expected to live out my days in a wheelchair. When I saw my orthopedic surgeon the following March, he told me to go home and say my prayers. Shortly afterward, I heard that a bus trip was being arranged for Father DiOrio's April 20 healing service at St. John's Church in Worcester. I just knew I had to be on that bus, so I stepped out in faith with my wife and two sisters, not knowing how I would tolerate the long ride.

While Father was praying over a woman in a wheelchair, I felt heat surge powerfully through my entire body. At that time I had never heard of burning in the Spirit. It was such a different experience for me. I felt as though my body was on fire. To be truthful, I was frightened. I did not know what was wrong with me and I was scared.

I was the fourth person Father called that day. He said there was a man with arthritis, a bad knee, and a cane in the audience. I knew it was me. I looked through the crowd and saw Father looking directly at me. When he opened his arms and said, "Come to me," I could not believe it. I said to myself, "Why me, Lord?" There were so many people there who were far more needing than I, yet the people, even those in wheelchairs, clapped their hands and rejoiced when I was called. Father told me to touch his hands. I was still on fire, but now I felt as though thousands of pins and needles were going through my body. As Father prayed, every bit of pain swiftly left. The tears flowed from my eyes as I stood before Father, and this wonderful man of God told me it was all right to cry. My tears were tears of joy. Here I was wanting only a blessing and I was being healed by God's loving power.

I am completely and totally free of all pain, and I praise, thank, and glorify Jesus every day of my life. No longer do I need any medication. My knee bends enough to allow me to drive. Not only did I receive a physical healing, but a spiritual one as well. My faith was renewed and strengthened. I pray daily for everyone who needs God's love. That is how I offer thanks to Jesus. I understand that Father DiOrio is God's instrument and I pray for him and his ministry every day. Through Father, God has changed our lives and we are much better people because of it. Since my healing I have become involved in the charismatic movement. I pray differently now, directly to Jesus. Every aspect of my life is improved, more open, and I am a new person in Christ. I know that I am never alone because Christ is always with me.

Marion speaks: I promised the Lord the day Bill fell that I would do whatever He asked of me, and that I would walk down any road He asked me to follow. I kept that promise, and despite all the odds against him, Bill survived. When Bill fell that February 24, 1980, I knew his arthritis had taken complete control of his body and I was sick with worry. Could I handle this? Would my nerves hold up? I was badly shaken, but the Lord stepped in and took all my fears, worries, and anxieties away from me that day at St. John's. I praise, thank, and glorify God each and every day for the wonderful gift we received.

And from his doctor, K. Prasad Srivastava, M.D., F.A.C.S., P.C., on May 6, 1986: "Mr. O'Brien has been completely free of his arthritic condition since April

20, 1980. Prior to that date, Mr. O'Brien was taking [medication] four times a day for his rheumatoid arthritis. As this condition no longer exists, it has not been necessary for me to prescribe any medication since that date."

PRAYER

Lord, You are continuously trying to communicate with us. You respect our bodies, but nothing is more important to You than our souls. What a wonderful God You are!

After You healed my body of rheumatoid arthritis, I more fully realized the value You place on my soul. Through Your servant, Father DiOrio, I truly accepted Your life into mine. Your simple healing touch brought my faith alive. Thank You, dear Lord, for introducing me to higher values, higher responsibilities.

Because of this renewed Christian vitality, I even pray differently now. It has improved my daily existence. Every aspect of my life seems brighter, clearer.

My grateful heart simply wants to sing out Your praises. In gratitude I rededicate my remaining earthly life to You and Your cause. Please continue to live within me and my dear wife and allow us to continue living within You. I praise and glorify You. Amen.

"Angry No More"

Anonymous

Healing: Rape

"Do you think you deserve credit for merely loving those who love you? Even the godless do that! And if you do good only to those who do you good—is that so wonderful? Even sinners do that much!" (Luke 6:32–33)

"Love your enemies! Be good to them! Lend to them! And don't be concerned about the fact that they won't repay. Then your reward from heaven will be very great, and you truly will be acting as sons of God: for he is kind to the unthankful and to those who are very wicked.

"Try to show as much compassion as your Father does." (Luke 6:35–36)

"Forgive us our trespasses as we forgive those who trespass against us. . . ." How often have we uttered those words without confronting ourselves with their true meaning? We ask God to forgive us, and tell Him we are forgiving everyone who has hurt us. Of course, keeping that promise is easier for some than for others. How much effort is required in forgiving someone who has been discourteous toward us? More effort is required to forgive the burglar who rummaged through our personal belongings and took our jewelry and television sets. But what of the man who robs us of something that never can be defined or replaced, who invades the body, strips the spirit, and weaves fear into our bodies and minds? How does a woman forgive a man who has raped her? Of course, she must. God does not command us to forgive just to have us obey Him. He knows that our pain and the resultant anger become a part of us, and all we say and do. Hatred permeates our souls, pushing out our pure love for God and His children. If we are to truly love God, then we must truly love even those who hate us and hurt us deeply. Jesus showed us how to love by loving the men who persecuted Him, drove nails through His flesh, and murdered Him.

With His help, a woman whom we will call Grace forgave the man who raped her. Today she walks not with fear, but with Jesus. She carried the burdensome hate for many years, from adolescence into adulthood, until she was healed by God through Father DiOrio. Because she has not yet told some family members what happened to her, we are honoring her request that her name and address not be disclosed.

Before my healing, every time there was a movie or show concerning rape, my blood ran cold. I would go deep inside myself and stay quiet for a long time. Whenever a man spoke out of turn to me, whether at work or on the street, my anger always caused me to insult him. I really had no respect for men, except for babies, young men, and priests. I was angry with men in general, and of course I hated the man who raped me when I was fifteen. He robbed me not only of my virginity, but he left me with emotional scars and took away my respect for men.

I sought out Father DiOrio, not for a healing, but just to learn. At his healing service one Friday night, Father DiOrio called forward all women who had been molested and raped. A cold chill ran through me and I groaned to God, "Oh no, Lord, not me. I don't need this healing. I buried it twenty-five years ago. Please don't make me do this. I am in the music ministry and all my friends are here." Now Father DiOrio was calling to the women for the last time, saying, "You will never have this chance again." Suddenly, a strange mood came over me, as though I was being dragged to the gallows by my own conscience. When Father made us get up before all those people and recount, in a few words, what had happened to us, I thought I would run away. I kept calm on the surface, but inside I was in torment. Then Father put his hands on me and I was slain in the Spirit. At first, I felt as though the only way to rid myself of the nightmare of it was to stay slain, and not have to face anyone ever again. But, I got up and went back to my seat in the music ministry. I couldn't look at anyone. The young bass player next to me put his arms around me and told me how proud he was of what I had just done. A singer seated behind me wrote me a note that said, "Remember, no one can cast the first stone." Later, as I played my guitar, I felt relaxed and mildly happy.

When the service was over, we went to the rectory to speak with Father DiOrio. He asked me how I felt and I told him I felt very light. I said no more because I was still feeling ashamed. When I left the rectory, I had a half-hour drive home. It was then that the Holy Spirit of God hit me like a mountain of emotion. I said, "Oh, God, I feel so good that I want to sing." I started singing, and all of a sudden there was so much love in my heart that I started to cry my heart out. I could hardly drive the car. I wiped away my tears and started to pray in tongues. Again, love flooded my soul and I burst out crying, "I forgive him, and I love him. Oh, how I love him. I am free, hallelujah!" At that point I realized just what had happened to me, and I was aware of a very deep compassion for the man who raped me. My eyes were brimming with tears again, and I couldn't stop marveling at how much I felt for this man.

A few days later, I noticed myself being kinder and more loving toward my son, my uncle, and the men in my prayer group. I knew that I had buried the past and was getting on with my present and future. I also stopped hating all men for what had happened to me. Now I look past their remarks and see their souls. I pray for them to change. I respect them more than ever. My hate is dried up and gone. My anger is not a problem anymore because when I am provoked I feel pity and forgiveness, not anger. I thank God for healing me at a time when I thought I had no need for emotional or spiritual healing. Praise God!

PRAYER

Dear, dear Lord, You were abused so awfully. I, too, to some degree, can identify with Your embarrassment. Perhaps it is more realistic to say that I can relate to Your pain because You identified with my suffering. It is true, dear Lord, that two hearts touch when pain abounds. Dear Lord, Your heart was open for all to look in. In that way Your heart was given to every man, woman, and child.

From Your wounded side You gave birth to Your people. Thank You for Your Sacred Heart. Thank You, Jesus, for Your joyous heart. Your overflowing joy makes me immune to unconscious slights, daily pinpricks, intentionally inflicted pains, and to the loneliness and drabness of life.

You allowed me to enter Your heart and bury my sadness in the joy of Your wounded love. Why are You so paradoxically giving? We hate, You love; we cry, You console; we live, You die.

Because You are always loving, I leave my gloom at the foot of the cross. There, at Calvary, I will drink deeply the red ripples of Your redemption, Your reconciliation, Your regeneration, Your righteousness. These are the roots of Your Resurrection. By these alone, my Lord and Savior, I was made whole again.

Thank You, Lord, for joy that surpasses human comprehension. Thank You for restoring me.

"Let Me Tell You What God Has Done for Me"

Rose Marie Truncellito
Ridgefield Park, New Jersey

*Healing: Disk pressing on nerves in
lower back, causing severe pain*

*O God, have pity, for I am trusting you! I will hide
beneath the shadow of your wings until this storm is
past. I will cry to the God of heaven who does such
wonders for me. He will send down help from
heaven to save me, because of his love and his faithfulness. . . . (Psalm 57:1–3)*

Pain is powerful. Sometimes it comes as irritating distraction. Other times it invades as an unrelenting presence permeating every aspect of life. In Rose Marie Truncellito's case, a damaged disk in her lower spine pressed on nerves in the spinal column, sending excruciating pain throughout her back and down her leg. It robbed her of the ability to perform routine tasks. No longer could she do her own grocery shopping or housework. How it must have scraped away at her self-esteem to watch others doing her work! The work God gives us, whether in the home or at a business, helps provide context for our lives. What we do for ourselves and for others is a part of who we are. As Rose Marie's pain intensified, the list of things she could do shrunk smaller and smaller. Walking, and even riding in the car, became agonizing experiences. She tried to push the pain away, but it throbbed through her body and oozed into every thought. It is hard to imagine that so much pain could result from a tiny pillowlike disk.

A disk is a small cushion of cartilage that sits between the vertebrae in the spinal column. When damaged, some of the soft, gelatinous material in the center of the disk pushes out and presses on the spinal nerves. Although many backaches are attributed to the so-called slipped disk, most actually are caused by muscle problems. In any case, back pain is a major medical problem in this country. It is the leading cause of lost time on the job. Medical treatments vary, and Rose Marie's first disk problem was corrected surgically. The second time the problem erupted, however, she was told that surgery might not relieve the pain. Faced with the possibility of never-ending pain, Rose Marie turned to the truly powerful Almighty God for help. He gave her more than she asked for, as she tells here.

In 1965 I had a disk problem in my lower back and I had an operation to remove part of the disk. I did very well after my back operation until 1981 when I started again with pains in my back and down my right leg and foot.

In 1982 I returned to the surgeon who did my operation. He had X rays of my back taken and said the pain was caused by a problem disk in my lower back, the same area as in 1965. My doctor said I would need another operation, which I did not want. He gave me medication for pain and on December 14, 1982, he sent me to the hospital for a depomedrol aristocort caudal injection. He said repeat surgery would be my only recourse if the injections into my spinal area did not work.

The injection was not effective.

I wanted to delay surgery because I had been through it already. I went to a chiropractor, but the treatment brought no relief. I called another doctor and asked for special injections called enzyme collagenese that were supposed to stop the pain by dissolving the matter around the disk that pressed on the nerves. I was told I was not a candidate for the injections because I had undergone back surgery in 1965.

Because I was not getting any better and was having difficulty walking, I went to a neurosurgeon in early 1984. I told him all that had happened so far and he sent me for a CAT scan, X rays, and electromyography. The neurosurgeon's diagnosis was the same as my original doctor's; a recurrence of the problem with the fifth disk in the lumbar region and the first in the sacral region. He prescribed painkillers, which I took three to four times a day.

Acting on my doctor's advice, I tried a conservative treatment of physical therapy. Heat, massage, and ultrasound treatments were administered three times a week at first, then less frequently for five or six months in all until October or November of 1984.

The therapy felt good, but within an hour or so I was the same, still with pain. The physical therapy was discontinued and I continued taking the painkillers.

By December 1984, my daughter helped me with my Christmas shopping. My husband helped with food shopping. My housework was being neglected. By January 1985, my husband was helping with housework because I could no longer drag the vacuum cleaner around the house or wash the floors. The medication was not freeing me from pain, not allowing me to function. Even walking a short distance was painful. I was doing very little in the house, just cooking and washing clothes.

I had seen Father Ralph A. DiOrio when I went on a church bus trip to Fordham University, New York, and another time at Madison Square Garden. I found out about the Apostolate of Healing in Massachusetts and sent for a schedule in December 1984. In March 1985, my husband took me to a healing service led by Father DiOrio in Worcester, Massachusetts. It was very uplifting.

Meanwhile, because I could not carry out usual everyday tasks, I contacted my doctor and told him I was ready to have the operation. He said he would be on vacation until a month from then and scheduled my appointment for July 25. I was devastated when he told me the recovery period after my operation would be nine months to a year. Also, he would have to do a fusion, which meant operating on my hip as well. The final blow was when he said he could not promise to make me well. Feeling depressed about the pain and upcoming operation, I called the apostolate for prayers.

When I thought about what my doctor had said

about no guarantee of making me well, I called and canceled my appointment. I felt God could make me well, even if the doctor couldn't. I called and got tickets for the July 28, 1985, service with Father Ralph A. DiOrio.

My husband, John, and friend, Pauline, traveled with me by car. We stayed overnight in Worcester, Massachusetts. I was disappointed because my name was not called on that day, although I really enjoyed the service with Father Ralph so much I knew I would come back for another service.

On our way home in the car, I was so hot (and I'm usually cool). I told my husband to put the air conditioner higher. My husband said it wasn't hot. I asked my friend, Pauline, if she was hot and she said no. I had thought everyone was hot. Then I got so excited and said, "Something good must be happening to my back because I am so hot."

We received a circular at the Worcester service, saying there were a few more openings for a trip to Lourdes, France, in August in less than two weeks. I made up my mind instantly to go to Lourdes with Father Ralph because if something good was happening to me, I wanted it to continue. My husband did not want to go, but my friend, Pauline, went with me.

At Lourdes we had a healing service with Father Ralph and also went into the bath waters twice. The first time on August 15, 1985. When I got into the cold water, I started to cough. The French ladies patted me on the back and talked to me in French, but I did not understand them. When I came out of the waters, I was tingling from head to toe. Also, while at Lourdes I felt hot. I felt wonderful and happy and I still did not know this was a part of healing. Then I met Joan from the Bronx, New York, at Lourdes and I was telling her about the feeling of heat and tingling and Joan said to me, "You must be getting a healing." I was astounded.

I loved my trip to Lourdes. The heat feeling continued for another four to six weeks at home. I felt good.

Since July 28, 1985, I have not taken any more medication, and I have not needed an operation or any treatment. Praise the Lord.

I had forgotten that Father Ralph had said at the Worcester services, that he doesn't have to call you or touch you, and that you may feel better when you go home. He had not called on me.

PRAYER

How awful pain is, dear Lord; how excruciating is its anguish. How often my pain-glazed eyes have looked out in search of healing! As I searched for relief, I found my quest in the steps leading to You.

You, O Christ, everlasting Searcher of Souls, recaptured my heart as You affirmed Your love for me through Your healing touch. How grateful one is to Him who removes the anguish of human pain!

When, in that last moment of hope I turned to You, I opened the veiled doors of my human life and You entered. Perhaps that is what pain is all about. Could it be that in the brokenness of our beings You are trying to break in with divine perspective, holy purity, and heavenly power? That must be the answer, because I have become much more attuned to Your daily presence and affection for me since You healed me. You used my hope to raise me to living faith. Oh, it is a terrible thing to lose hope!

My prayer is one of gratitude, immense gratitude for the warm feelings Your healing love laid upon my fevered body. Those divine healing hands *brought me new life as the Holy Spirit expelled the evil of suffering pain.*

I thank You, Lord, for healing and restoration. Our times definitely are in Your hands. Thank You, Lord, for still healing as You did long ago in Palestinian days.

Thank you for answering our prayer, born of our faith and offered in trusted hope, blessed in Your love. O Great Divine Physician, praise to Your name!

"Leave Your Burdens at the Foot of the Cross"

Betty McCauley
Northford, Connecticut

Healing: Inner healing

O Lord, don't hold back your tender mercies from me! My only hope is in your love and faithfulness. Otherwise I perish, for problems far too big for me to solve are piled higher than my head. . . . (Psalm 40:11–12)

Do you ever have so much on your mind that you feel unrelenting pressure weighing against you on all sides? You try to sort your thoughts and make decisions, but anxiety and fear surround reason, squeezing it into oblivion. You can't relax. You are never at ease.

Perhaps Betty McCauley's story will help you.

I believe in the power of God and that God heals.

On August 3, 1986, I was sitting in the balcony of Worcester Auditorium in Massachusetts. It was my first time at a healing service and I didn't know quite what to expect. I couldn't concentrate because of an impending divorce, possible loss of my home, and a career change.

At the service, Father DiOrio's voice was soothing, but for the most part the meaning of the words escaped me. About an hour into the service I felt a strong tingling sensation in both feet. It radiated up to my knees. I looked around. No one else acted like anything unusual was happening. About a half hour later, Father DiOrio announced that an inner healing would start with a strong sensation in one part of the body followed by a feeling of being hot. Then, when Father said it was all right to cry, all the tears I had been holding back flowed freely. I sobbed, then I got very hot. I felt as though I was standing near a fire. This heat continued throughout the time Father was praying for inner healings. When Father said the inner healing was complete, I felt totally drained and at peace.

Since that day I have been able to think clearly, concentrate, and make decisions.

I believe in the power of God and that He heals.

PRAYER

Dear Lord, peace is so precious. For some people it has become a rare commodity, almost a stranger. Why would anyone forfeit it so easily? How predictable we humans can be. How we complicate ourselves.

Peace, on the other hand, is so tranquil. A peaceful soul should not be easily surrendered. Peace is Your gift to us. Thank You, Lord.

I thank You for truth and for Your constant love even when we make the wrong choices. You are an uplifter. Even when we are down in the mud, we need only to look up at You. What a marvelous insight that is; to look up, never down!

Really, when You see us suffering in human brokenness, I guess You must ask Yourself, "Why don't they return to Me?"

Because You are a God of wonder, You filled my inner need with the magnificent You!

Thank You. Your grace alone helped me bring out the best of me which was to be. When You touched me with inner healing, You, dear Master, gave me a wonderful sign and wonder. You gave me a miracle of love!

"Because God Loves, My Daughter Lives"

Amber Dopieralski
Darrington, Washington

Healing: Axillary tumor

But I will send you the Comforter—the Holy Spirit, the source of all truth. He will come to you from the Father and will tell you about me. And you also must tell everyone about me, because you have been with me from the beginning.

(John 15:26–27)

Today Carmen Dopieralski describes her daughter, Amber, as a normal, healthy sixteen-year-old with a God-given gift for playing the piano. Back in 1979, however, when Amber was only eight years old, she was not the picture of health her mother depicts now.

Silently, sneakingly, illness crept into Amber, making her sicker and sicker. So subtle was the illness that her parents did not realize how sick their daughter was until it was almost too late. As Amber recalls, her underarm hurt so much that she did not want to participate in gym class but for a long time no one believed her complaint was valid.

Desperate, the Dopieralskis turned to God through Father DiOrio's radio show, "Hour of Healing." Today Amber remembers little about her illness, but she has not forgotten the God who healed her. She also agreed to have her story told so other young people will realize the friend they have in God. In fact, this active sixteen-year-old is planning a pilgrimage to Rome as an act of commitment to God the Father.

Mrs. Dopieralski remembers her daughter's ordeal well and glorifies God by sharing it with you.

Amber started having pain under her right arm in September of 1979. She couldn't do the exercises in her physical education class in school and seemed to lose some of her color. I remember, however, that in September Amber still had some of the special spark that was so characteristic of her.

Several weeks before Halloween, Amber began to run slight fevers and her color had a gray hue. She missed some days at school and was always complaining of being too warm, even when the weather was cold. She used to lie on the floor instead of playing, and she was growing thinner.

As a mother, I must admit that at first I believed Amber was just a complainer, although that was not consistent with her nature. Finally, after many days of Amber not seeming like herself, I took her to a nurse practitioner. By this time a small walnut-sized lump had appeared under Amber's right arm. She was treated for a virus and antibiotics were prescribed for ten days. Amber was still sick after she had been taking the medicine for five days. My mother, who lives next door, kept saying that Amber was not well, but I simply replied that the medicine needed more time to work. I just couldn't or wouldn't believe that my Amber was as sick as she was.

Sometime before the middle of November, I was visiting with my sister in the kitchen. It was very early in the morning, before 7 A.M., and I suddenly realized that Amber, my baby, could be seriously ill. She was lying on the living room floor. She was so thin, so gray, and her eyes were rolled back. Amber looked very far away and her skin was so hot to the touch that it felt like it was on fire. My sister suggested that I call the children's hospital and a staff doctor agreed to see her that day. By this time the lump had grown as large as an egg.

Once again Amber was given antibiotics, but the lump remained and grew to half the size of an orange. The doctors told us they suspected lymphatic cancer, a cancer that already would have spread to other organs. That's when it hit me—Amber was dying.

My mother had attended a healing service held by Father Ralph A. DiOrio in Minnesota. She told me about his radio program and advised me to call him. My sister dialed the telephone for me, then I spoke to Father DiOrio. He told me to call Amber to the phone and he said he was feeling a pain under his right arm.

Acting on his instructions, I placed my hand on the growth under Amber's arm and prayed with him. I remember crying and saying, "Thank you, Jesus." My hand got so hot that it seemed to melt into Amber's arm. I can't explain the heat. Amber said, "It's hot. It's hot," then she fell over. When she fell she hit her head on a large heavy statue but she was not hurt. Father DiOrio told us to leave her alone, so we did not move her. Father said, "What was bothering Amber is no more." Amber lay down for twenty minutes, then sat up and said she wanted to color. I cried because I was happy that she wanted to play. She told me God had taken her bump away, and I truly believe that the lump matter later removed was different from what would have been found before the healing.

On November 30 Amber was operated on. The doctor told me later that the whole operating room was in jubilation at what they found. As the laboratory report states, the doctors have no idea what the lump was. They analyzed the decayed matter and called it surprising, a red herring comprised of substances they had not seen before. The important thing is that the lump was not lymphatic cancer, was not cancer at all, and Amber is well.

God healed my daughter. I pray to God that I have communicated the truly intense times we went through. As we live our lives now, we continually thank God for each of Amber's new days.

PRAYER

Dear Lord, You know how shy I am at times, but somehow I am never at a loss for words when I'm praying to You. It was so hard for my mother to realize I was sick. Perhaps subconsciously she believed she could not bear for her child's life to be slipping away. Thank You for telling my mother I was dangerously ill, and thank You for standing by her. When You healed me, You not only restored my health and liveliness, but also spared my mother grief.

You astounded the doctors, but not my mother. Sure, she and I are more grateful than we can say, but we know the infinite bounds of Your miracles and power. We know You can do anything, things that mere mortals cannot even dream up.

Those of us who really enjoy the gift of faith are never foolish or ridiculous in our hope. Only the fool says within his heart, "There is no God." The lucky ones realize He is still living among us. He walks and talks to us through His chosen earthly vessels. How blessed we are in these modern times to be instructed by Him still. Your Son, Jesus, certainly lives with us today as He did many years ago and as He will forever. He is a radiance to all who experience Him. Jesus was not just any man. He was and is the true Jesus.

"Faith Undaunted"

Michael D. Flanagan, Jr.
Worcester, Massachusetts

Healing: Encephalitis

*Because the Lord is my Shepherd, I have everything
I need! (Psalm 23:1)*

Ask Betty and Michael Flanagan, Sr., how they came to work on Father DiOrio's prayer line once a week and you will hear a beautiful, touching, miraculous story. The Flanagans know the pain and desperation parents feel when they ask for prayers for their children. They understand the need to know that someone has survived the unsurvivable, has beaten the odds and delighted the doctors by miraculously staying alive. In early summer of 1985 when their son Michael was twelve years old, he suddenly was afflicted by encephalitis, an acute swelling of the brain. Then, as now, no cause for the onset in Michael's case is known. Saying her only emotion was fear, Mrs. Flanagan recalls turning to the prayer line. "I say to myself, I want someone else to know that, yes, things can turn around," she said. "I clung to anything, any ounce of hope. I needed to know that someone else had survived, had come out of a coma."

Mrs. Flanagan also will tell you that she and her husband are different now than they were before their son's brush with death. "Oh, we were never materialistic and we always had faith, but now we have more faith. Before, perhaps we would think about what we didn't have sometimes, or wish momentarily that we had more. Now we never feel that way. Our priorities are different, but we have not changed our lives. When we look at Michael, we know we have everything."

The time the Flanagans put in answering calls and praying with people is purely voluntary in every way. "We made no bargains for Michael. As we stood beside Father DiOrio as he prayed, I thought to myself that I would work for this man. We started in January 1986 and we go because we want to, not because we feel obliged."

Mrs. Flanagan agreed to share Michael's story

*here for much the same reason she works the prayer
line, to share the miracle, extend hope, and glorify God.*

I have often said that I wish I could write a book
on the happenings in our lives during the six months
of Michael's illness. We look back on it and still get
the chills thinking about the bizarre chain of events
that took place.

It began on a normal day in June with twelve-
year-old Michael playing outside with friends. He
came into the house complaining, or should I say, puz-
zled, by a slight twitching on one side of his face. Thus
began Michael's saga. He was tested at St. Vincent's
Hospital in Worcester, then returned home where he
worsened. As advised, we brought Michael to the University of Massachusetts Hospital in Worcester.

The physicians at U. Mass. Hospital decided to
place Michael in a drug-induced coma because it apparently was the only way to control the seizures. This
is when our heartache really began. Soon after he was
placed in the coma, within perhaps a few days, we
were told that Michael could not be brought out of the
coma. The doctor told us that Michael was showing
flat brain waves; that is to say that they could not
detect any brain activity. At that point we were told
our son would die within a day or two.

Desperate and very scared, we called Father Di-
Orio's prayer line and were comforted. I must say that
although I am sure my hopes faltered at times, my
faith did not. I always knew that God was with us and
I was almost always certain that Michael would survive despite the medical prognosis. On the very evening of July 5, when we were told Michael had only a
day or two to live, I was sitting in the hospital waiting
room when my friend pointed out the window and
told me that Father DiOrio was on his way in. I can't

describe the experience of watching that priest walk across the parking lot. I'll never forget it. There was just something special about him. I remember thinking that now everything would be all right.

Father DiOrio, his assistant Virginia McNiff, another assistant, two close relatives, and my husband and I went to Michael's room and we all prayed together. It was an indescribable feeling knowing Father was there, right there. I did not expect Michael to sit right up then, and Father said it might take time. He was right. It took about five weeks. After Father prayed with us, he prayed over another child, then gave a general blessing to everyone in the ward.

I had some bad days during the long weeks that followed, but I really always was confident that Michael would get better. Sometimes we were looked at almost strangely because we had such faith. Although no one except Father DiOrio gave us any reason to hope, I didn't give up. Out of all the days that were given to us as hopeless, I cannot say that I shared those feelings each of those days, although probably for a couple of them I did.

About a week after Father's visit, on a Tuesday or Wednesday, Michael's lungs collapsed and his doctor said he absolutely needed a miracle or Michael would not survive. I remember his doctor sitting and crying with us because he felt so bad. He was very close to Michael because he spent so much time with him. I had never been to one of Father's healing services because I simply spent all my time in the hospital with Michael. Now, however, my husband and I decided to go to the chapel at the Apostolate of Prayer for the noon holy hour on Friday, just a few days after the bad news. Father DiOrio happened to be there and he said Mass. We did not speak to him that day and returned to the hospital right after Mass. We had not been in the hospital for five minutes when the doctor told us that he did not understand why, but Michael's lung condition had improved slightly. From that time on Michael just got better and better, and about a week after our chapel visit he opened his eyes and awoke from the coma. He came to fully as though he had been merely asleep.

Oh, he had respiratory problems to be dealt with after that, as well as a circulation problem which resulted in the loss of his left foot, but from that moment on he was alive and alert and mentally our old Michael again, and that is all that matters. You see, what Father DiOrio said about results not always happening immediately was so true in Michael's case. We hung onto those words and to the words of the prayer line staff. We always were uplifted as we prayed, even on our most dismal days in the prayer house.

We were always a faith-filled family, or should I say my husband and I were. My children were like most children, going to church but not quite understanding it all. But, oh, how this has all changed. You can see it in them daily. They, like us, now know the power of prayer and the importance of faith. You see, when God saved Michael, he did not just save one child, he saved a family.

I must say that Michael has been an inspiration to lots of people. He has helped restore the faith and hope of many. His attitude is especially inspirational because this child has never once uttered a complaint and has a smile on his face most every time you look at him. I, for one, look at him constantly and thank God every time. You know, during the time that Michael was sick people just came out from all over; people we knew and people we had never met. We only knew our priest at church, but so many priests came to the hospital to see him that the nurses called Michael's room the Vatican. When it was all over and Michael was home, we held a special Mass of Thanksgiving at our church at a time when there were no scheduled masses. We just had to say thank you to everyone. I think most of the priests who had visited the hospital were on the altar. Everyone came; the church was overflowing. We never take Michael to the doctor without people being amazed that he is alive. It's truly a miracle. It really is.

Now, everything is going along as normally as can be. Michael came home in November 1985 with help from a visiting nurse. At first he was tutored at home, then he returned to school in September 1986. Now he is working on a return to sports and has joined the basketball team. We don't know how it will work out, but he is giving it a try. There have been days when I've wondered about the cause of the encephalitis and worried that I might be doing something wrong, but I can't drive myself crazy with that. I am just so happy we have him. It really is like a bad dream with a happy ending.

PRAYER

Tender was the pain. Gracious was the blessing. Such was our experience as simple, loving parents. To whom could we turn in our anguish as we watched our son wither away? All we had was our hope and our faith. We knew that You, dear God, were not a faraway, impersonal deity hidden from us by clouds.

What did our heritage of faith bring to us? Slowly, step by step, You strengthened Your miracle love within our lives. You dispelled the darkness and made us worthy to be taught by You personally. Your arrival was no coincidence.

In those last hours Your radiance came to us through faith alone. We thank You for this faith. Faith became vision as You touched our eyes just as You did when You walked as a man among men. Now You are with us sacramentally, not just historically. You are a true God! You are not just a man. You made the blind see, the lame walk, and the deaf hear. You cleansed the lepers, and by a simple command You raised the dead back to life.

We thank you for an enhanced appreciation of the gifts of life and supportive friendship. What tremendous, powerful graces there are: Life and Friends! Compassion and Support! These, dear Lord, are You.

We, like many other humans, sometimes feel sorry for ourselves when life seems to break its promises to us. In times of tragedy many would cry out with Isaiah as in chapter 63, verse 3: "I have trodden the winepress alone." Some of us, however, realize that Jesus intercedes in the eleventh hour for the glory of his Father and the winning of souls.

We thank You, dear God, for being everything to us. We thank You for the many people who did all that was humanly possible for us. When mortals could do no more, You walked the hospital corridors unobtrusively and laid Your healing hand upon our son.

This is our miracle story, a true story that we will witness to all the world for Your glory. We publicly thank You as we rejoice in the power of faith.

A mighty victory has been won by Your wonderful power and holiness.

"No More Medicine"

Stacie Jaksha
Butte, Montana

*Healing: Chronic kidney
and bladder infections*

*"O righteous Father, the world doesn't know you,
but I do; and these disciples know you sent me. And
I have revealed you to them, and will keep on re-
vealing you so that the mighty love you have for me
may be in them, and I in them." (John 17:25–26)*

"Enjoy yourself now. These are the best years of your life." Parents repeat these words to their children frequently, but it is doubtful that children really believe them. It is the nature of youth to look forward to the freedom of adulthood.

It is childhood, however, that usually offers true opportunities for uninhibited, unencumbered fun. Unfortunately, burdens sometimes squeeze laughter and spontaneity out of the childhood years.

For Stacie Jaksha, it was her health, not her child-like spirit, that dictated daily activities until she was almost thirteen years old. Between bouts of illness Stacie felt well and could play, but when periodic bladder and kidney infections sapped her strength and made her feel sick, fun was impossible.

Fortunately for Stacie, her mother has an open mind and listens to her daughter. Stacie had learned a great deal about Father DiOrio from her cousin, so when her cousin had extra tickets to a service at the Butte Civic Center in Montana, Stacie made up her mind to go. She knew God would heal her through the humble priest. With Stacie's permission, her mother, Sandra, testifies to the healing.

When Stacie was seven months old, she started running fevers, 104 to 105 degrees, fairly regularly. The doctors checked her for all kinds of things at that time and discovered Stacie had a bladder infection. They ran another test and discovered that Stacie's left kidney is quite a bit larger than her right kidney. That is because she has hemihypertrophy, which means that the entire left side of her body, including internal organs, is larger than the right side of her body.

Daily medication was prescribed for Stacie, as well as antibiotics that she took whenever she got bladder and kidney infections. Stacie's urine was analyzed periodically and it usually showed infection and sometimes had blood in it. Until she was healed, the longest time I remember Stacie not taking medicine was six days.

Over the years Stacie missed school whenever she got a bad infection and her fever went up, and she was hospitalized several times. When she was about six years old she was admitted to the University Hospital in Salt Lake City, Utah, for extensive tests to see if there was an operation or anything that could be done to help Stacie. They determined there was nothing permanent they could do for her. They increased her medicine and told her she probably would have to take it for the rest of her life.

When Stacie got the infections, she had a lot of low-back pain and quite a bit of pain in her abdomen. She became listless and sick. She was so tired of being sick. She used to feel embarrassed, too, because she had to take the medicine at school. Stacie said the medicine tasted "gross" and some of the pills were so large they used to get stuck in her throat.

When Stacie got the tickets to go to Father Di-Orio's healing service, she really believed that was it. She was going to be healed and not feel sick anymore. She said, "I know I will be healed. I can feel it." When she went to the service on October 6, 1985, she was taking an antibiotic twice a day. She was sick with a temperature of 103 degrees. During the service she told me, "When I leave here, I won't have to take the medicine anymore."

The day after the service Stacie broke out in hives. I could not reach her doctor, so I spoke to the doctor on call and she advised us to stop the medication. At that point Stacie had only been on the medication for a few days and it takes about two weeks for her bouts of infection to clear.

On October 11 her physician ran urine tests and found no trace of infection. In fact, Stacie has not had any urinary tract infections at all since she was healed, as the doctor mentioned in his letter. Stacie told me, "I know I'm not sick anymore. I'm not going to get sick anymore, so don't waste your money on doctors." The doctors tested Stacie's urine every month until February 1986 and still found it clear. Now she just has regular checkups, but until the healing her urine had to be checked every two weeks to a month, depending on her health.

Stacie believes God healed her through Father DiOrio and I have to believe it, too. We are just ordinary people. We go to church on Sunday, but we were never extremely religious. Now, we no longer worry about Stacie getting sick and our faith is stronger.

Stacie is excited about her healing and grateful that she is free to live normally. Stacie wrote to Father DiOrio, "I am doing just great. Thank you."

PRAYER

Dear Jesus, this is Stacie. Many times we humans need simply to talk because answers come to us as we speak to You.

Lord, I talk to You an awful lot and I am especially grateful that You never tire of hearing me. I was so sick for such a long time. You know how suffering inflicts ugliness. The consequences seem endless.

Before I was healed I had heard of miracles. They were happy stories and everyone likes happy stories. It seems, though, that miracles only hap-

pened at Christmas and never to anyone I knew. Miracles, to be honest, sounded like they would be nice if only they really happened. A lot of people think this way.

One day, dear Jesus, You came to our hearts in a very special way. You came as a Divine Helper to people in need. You came because You love us, and as You helped us Your love became a miracle. You came to change the sad way people think, and to give us a joyous perspective. You chose to come to us through Father Ralph, a funnel of Your miracle love. Like a child whose heart glows for the extraordinary, I received a miracle! That's my story, a miracle of God's love!

Thank You, dear Jesus. The rest of my life is Yours.

"No Need Is Too Small"

Adé Lewis
Castries, St. Lucia, West Indies

Healing: Amputated fingertip regrown

But thanks be to God! For through what Christ has done, he has triumphed over us so that now wherever we go he uses us to tell others about the Lord and to spread the Gospel like a sweet perfume.

As far as God is concerned, there is a sweet, wholesome fragrance in our lives. It is the fragrance of Christ within us, an aroma to both the saved and the unsaved all around us. To those who are not being saved, we seem a fearful smell of death and doom, while to those who know Christ we are a life-giving perfume. But who is adequate for such a task as this? Only those who, like ourselves, are men of integrity, sent by God, speaking with Christ's power, with God's eye upon us. We are not like those hucksters—and there are many of them—whose idea in getting out the Gospel is to make a good living out of it. (2 Corinthians 2:14–17)

*During the summer of 1986, I had the privilege of serv-
ing some of the neediest of God's children at several
healing services in Castries, St. Lucia, in the West Indies. It was my first visit to the West Indies when I was
asked to prepare the people for a visit from His Holiness, Pope John Paul II.*

*God's faithful and hopeful children ventured to
services by whatever means available. The crippled hob-
bled wearily to hear God's word. Mothers and fathers
carried their sick children along dusty dirt roads to the
hot, crowded buildings. Their faith reached out to Jesus
and he showered them with many blessings. Lilith
Dalphinis-Lewis tells the touching story of her son Adé's
healing. May it touch your heart as it has touched
mine.*

On the feast of Corpus Christi in May, 1986, Adé,
my son, had a serious accident. His left finger was
effectively amputated in a bedroom door—acciden-
tally—by the girl who was looking after him while my
husband and I worked. Paula, who also is his god-
mother, did not see him and slammed the door very
hard on his finger. Adé was then less than three
months away from his second birthday. He is our only
child. He did not lose a lot of finger. He lost the tip
and a bit of bone. However, the nail was ripped out at
the root and attached, with its entire root, to the piece
of his finger which fell to the floor.

Surprisingly, I managed to remain calm, and so
did my husband. Paula, Adé, my husband, and I managed to do all the right things. We put the piece of
Adé's finger in a cup of water and rushed it with him

to the St. Jude Hospital. We were hoping that the doctors might be able to sew it back on.

Naturally, Adé was experiencing a lot of pain and shock. His eyes rolled as he screamed over and over, "Paula! Paula! Paula!"

We were lucky that almost as soon as we arrived the doctor came into the emergency room. Adé had to be wrapped very tightly in a sheet to prevent him from wriggling. My husband and I also held him and talked to him; we were trying to comfort him. I asked the doctor whether he could put Adé to sleep to work on the finger. He said, however, that an injection would suffice. At that point, my knees almost gave way underneath me—thinking about what Adé was feeling. I also was busy negotiating with the doctor about stitching the last piece back on. I say negotiating but I really was begging him to try and sew it back on. The doctor explained, very kindly, that the probability of rejection was high with a fingertip and probably would only cause further complications in the long run. He also explained that the hospital did not have the equipment or facilities for microsurgery. Again my knees nearly failed me. Adé was still screaming and looking frantically from the doctor and nurse to us.

I had to try to comfort him. I glanced up and saw a crucifix on the wall and called upon Jesus to assist. I said the "Hail Mary" and the "Our Father" and then I started to sing the song I used to sing to Adé when he was newborn, "Mr. Blue, Mr. Blue, God Loves You, Mr. Blue." Adé fell asleep almost immediately. This saved him from a lot of additional pain, so I felt relieved. My husband was quietly there, holding Adé's hand and patting it.

The doctor sliced the skin on both sides of the finger and pulled as much skin as he could up and over the open wound. There was not enough skin to cover it over. It looked ugly. Slicing both sides like that would help give the finger a shape when it healed.

I accepted that the piece of finger was not going to be stitched back on, then I asked about the fingernail. Would it grow back? I again pleaded with the doctor. Again, his answer was hard to accept. "Probably not" because the root was pulled out, he explained. I was shocked.

I did not start to cry until we were out of the emergency room, but the sight and state of Paula prevented me from giving way to further tears until later. Paula was in a state. We drove home quietly. Adé asked for some fish sticks to eat. We gave him some painkilling medicine and he soon fell asleep again. God was merciful toward him.

Paula took a scrubbing brush and basin to clean the blood from the floor, then broke down in tears again. I had to comfort her. She has looked after Adé, lovingly, since he was almost six months old. I knew it was an accident.

Later on, my husband, who is very practical and down-to-earth, reminded me that it was unfortunate that it had happened and there was nothing we could do about it. It would be best now to get some rest, go to sleep. This we did. However, I could not sleep. I went into the kitchen and took a statuette of the Blessed Virgin. I placed it on a trunk near the bed, lit a candle, and I prayed silently to our Holy Mother. I prayed five decades of the rosary, then fell asleep begging Mary and Jesus to help Adé.

The next day we had an early appointment with Dr. Price at the hospital. He showed us how to clean and dress the finger and cautioned us that it would not heal in a hurry. By the end of June, Adé's finger was still not fully healed. It still looked very nasty. I kept up my prayers daily. I had become very depressed and wept almost at the drop of a hat. I would remember the sound of the door, the way he screamed, the piece of finger.

Luckily for me, I had a very dear friend who was a Catholic nun. She had taught my husband and me how to keep a prayer journal. Really, it is a way of praying by writing instead of talking aloud to God. I had been doing this for well over a year before the accident.

One night while my husband and child slept, I sat at my kitchen table, praying by writing. I opened the Bible to the words, "It is vain for you to eat the bread of sorrow." I knew that our Lord was telling me to pull myself together and not be so morose. From that moment my burden felt lighter. I was still hurt about the accident, but I no longer was carrying it around my neck like a millstone! God is good. I continued to take my problems and worries to Mary by candlelight before falling asleep. I prayed that Adé would grow a fingernail so that his finger would not appear deformed. Sometimes my prayer was frantic! I was becoming almost obsessed, begging Mary for a fingernail for Adé. Every day my husband and I dressed the finger. There definitely was no sign of a fingernail. I had almost resigned myself to Adé's injured finger never having a fingernail.

I am a secondary school teacher. One day a friend of mine who was seriously contemplating becoming a nun (she has since entered an order) told me that a Roman Catholic American priest, through whom Jesus heals, was planning to visit St. Lucia soon to prepare people for the Pope's visit. This was in June. Without knowing any details, I told her I believed God healed through this man. I asked her to make sure to get me two tickets to the healing service. I would pray with this priest for a fingernail for Adé! I felt optimistic. I counted the days.

I rushed home after school to tell my husband

about my good news. He thought that I was a real twit. This priest must be some kind of phony, he thought. When my husband learned that I was going to ask for a fingernail, he laughed at me and assured me that he was not going to attend the service and see me make a fool of myself in public! I was stubborn about attending the service, alone if necessary.

In the end, my husband went against his instincts and on the date of the priest's visit (I did not know his name then) he accompanied Adé and me to the church. Imagine how my heart sank when we arrived at the church one hour early to find it packed. We were lucky to find seats right at the back. My expectations of a half-empty church and the attention of this "healing priest" were dashed.

My friend, Jane, was on the altar leading the recitation of the rosary. The service was very different from any church service I had ever attended. Father Ralph effectively guided the congregation of people of many different religions into simple but direct prayer to God. Very often the congregation uttered many phrases directly from scripture, including "Oh, Jesus, Son of David, I love you!"

I did not really participate in the service as fully as I would have liked to. The crowd was dense; the heat unbearable. Adé was extremely restless. He was playing up. That night I saw with my own two eyes—blind people saw! The deaf heard! Crippled people walked! It was amazing. It showed us all that God is very much alive.

I waited patiently, thinking this holy man would know about my son and his need for a fingernail. I expected to be called forward to the altar. The service was ending. I felt heartbroken, almost frantic. He wouldn't go without healing Adé, would he? It seemed then that he would. My fingernail problem, it seemed, was not as big as those of the people receiving healings. If I could only get to the front of the church, surely the Holy Spirit would see Adé's need. I knew my husband, who is very conservative, would not tolerate me showing us up in public. Then Adé solved the problem for me. He was so hot that I had taken off his shirt. He ran away from me through the crowd, toward the altar! I followed him, for once thankful that he is occasionally troublesome.

I caught up with him at the front of the church. The second part of the solution was Jane, sitting at the front of the church with an empty seat beside her. I sat quickly in it and we smiled at each other. I knew she was praying for us.

Very soon, a mother sent her child up to Father Ralph, unrequested. Then another mother took an infant in her arms and sought healing. This gave me the courage to go, unrequested, up to the altar. Then something happened to me. A force compelled me to kneel down. Father Ralph held Adé's wrist. "It's his finger, not his wrist," I thought. But, as it turned out, this was all Father needed to do.

Rapidly now the service was ending, but I felt that I had made it. Soon the Blessed Sacrament was exposed. The Bishop, clergy, and Father Ralph passed through the aisles blessing everyone. On the way back to the altar, Father Ralph stopped at my row of seats. He bent over my head and Adé's, who was on my lap, and gave something to Jane. I felt such a presence that I trembled in awe. This man was really a vehicle of God. How humbly he implored all of us not to thank him but to thank God. He was nothing but an instrument, he insisted. He begged all of us to go to our homes and pray and read the Gospels frequently. Some would be healed instantly, some later, but we should continue to pray for healing if it had not occurred immediately.

We arrived home exhausted. I eagerly took Adé's

bandage off. "Was that little bit of white there before?" I showed my husband the nail coming through. He insisted that we were all tired, that I was tired and should go to bed and stop imagining things. Every day the little white bit came through a little bit more. Eventually, even a skeptic had to admit it was a nail! Within a few days we threw away all the dressings. The finger had healed beautifully and did not even look as if it had been cut. It is now only slightly shorter than the right index finger. I got more than the fingernail I had begged Mary and Jesus for. Gradually Adé learned to use his finger again, and only a close inspection would indicate that any accident had ever occurred.

How happy I have felt since then. It is as though the accident never happened. The experience rapidly accelerated my desire to maintain and deepen my relationship with God. I want to pray more, to make God the center of my life, to do something more about my faith. I desire to love and trust Mary even more. I pray that Jesus will strengthen me and my family in His love always. My heart is full of love, respect, and awe for Father Ralph, who will never accept a compliment. Thanks and praise be to God always. Praise be to our Heavenly Father always for choosing Father Ralph as His instrument. I will never forget Father or cease to pray for him as he journeys to the five continents doing God's will.

PRAYER

> Dear Lord, hear my prayer. I come to You through the heart of Your dear mother, Mary. Mary is not the church's creation, for humans could never begin to comprehend the depth of her holiness. Your creations are creations of mystery.

You decided she would be born and give birth to Your son. It was Your plan from all eternity. I adore Your immense intelligence.

Oh, how I admire Your wisdom and love!

With a mother's sentiments, not unlike Your mother's, I utter my prayer of gratitude. Just as Your mother anguished over Your wounds, I, on a much smaller scale, cried over my own son's wounded finger. How totally a mother suffers when she sees her child in pain. Joined to his heart, she feels his pain and cries his tears.

Dear Mother Mary, my spiritual and heavenly mother, accept my sentiments, my heart, my mind, my all. Mingle these as one with yours. And with my heart and hand in yours, help me offer infinite gratitude for the healing of my son Adé's amputated finger.

What a miracle! Could anyone imagine that a fingertip, bone, and root would be replaced, not by man's ingenuity, but by God's grace.

Mary, while I watched my son in excruciating pain you were with me and we were one. Like you, I held my grief inside and stood by my child as you stood by yours in His time of need. My prayers and devotions to you, dear Mother, became my strength, my inspiration to be bold enough to ask your Son for nothing less than a miracle.

O Mary, let us adequately thank your Son together.

How blessed I am to see a miracle like this! Because he is a miracle child I offer him anew to you in service to your Son.

"I Walk with the Lord"

Rose Roxanne Ladd
Wilbraham, Massachusetts

Healing: Spiritual

I will extol Thee, my God, O King;
And I will bless Thy name forever and ever.
Every day I will bless Thee,
And I will praise thy name forever and ever.
Great is the Lord, and highly to be praised;
And His greatness is unsearchable.
One generation shall praise Thy works to another,
And shall declare Thy mighty acts.
On the glorious splendor of Thy majesty,
And on Thy wonderful works, I will meditate.
And men shall speak of the power of Thine awesome
   acts;
And I will tell of Thy greatness.
They shall eagerly utter the memory of Thine
   abundant goodness,
And shall shout joyfully of Thy righteousness.

(Psalm 145:1–7)

Who can describe a mother's love for her child? As mothers we try, but only another mother really understands the love that lives within mothers for their children. It is who we are. When our children call to us we go to them, not only because they want us, but because we need to be with them. And we thank God that they have turned to us. It was this love for her child that set Rose Roxanne on a torturous journey to death's door, a journey that ultimately would lead her to never-ending joy.

Many of you will cry with Roxanne as she tells you her story, tears of pain followed by tears of joy. When you finish we hope that you will rejoice with her, not only because she is alive, but because Christ is alive within her.

On November 5, 1985, the telephone in the office rang. It was my daughter and she was crying. She had to go into the hospital and she wanted me to come to Florida to be with her. She is my only child and I love her very much, so naturally I said, "Yes, I'll come. I'll get a plane down as soon as I can." I made arrangements to leave the office and go home, get some clothes, and book a flight to Florida.

When I left the office that morning, it was very foggy, drizzly, and rainy. It was very hard to see. Instead of following my usual course home, I opted to drive a shorter route to avoid traffic and save time. I remember the car in front of me. The man was wearing a white felt hat. That hat stuck in my memory because it reminded me of a picture of my grandfather wearing a similar but gray felt hat. The picture hung on my mother's wall when I was a young child. Anyway, as I drove along Route 20 I tried to pass this man's car because he was driving too slowly. But every time I tried to pass him he picked up speed so I couldn't get by. Then, when I pulled back in behind him, he slowed down. Then, when I tried to pass him again, he picked up speed and pulled in front of me. He continued this seesaw game for quite a while. The driver behind me started to toot impatiently, so I waved him on, saying, "Go ahead, pass me." As he passed me and passed the other car, he made a fist at the man in front of me, who was oblivious to everything. It appeared that he was either deep in conversation or arguing with the person beside him. He simply was not paying attention to the road or other drivers. Again, I tried to pass him, but it was difficult because he continued to slow down, then pick up speed. The last time I tried, I remember that I was alongside him and he kept coming at me, pulling to the side into my right fender, it seemed. That's all I remember.

They tell me that an eighteen-wheel trailer truck went over the top of my car, crushing it flat. I was thrown at least seventy feet from the car. The ambulance brought me to Harrington Memorial Hospital in Southbridge, but because I was critically injured I was transferred to the University of Massachusetts Hospital in Worcester. At Harrington, my husband was told that I probably would not make it. My injuries included two broken legs, two broken arms, and a broken collarbone. Almost all my ribs were broken. My pelvic girdle was cracked. I had a gash on the back of my head and a huge chunk of flesh was missing from the back of my leg.

The doctors cut my throat and inserted an umbrella to strain my blood so no clots would travel to my heart or brain. After putting me back together, the doctors called my husband into the office and told him that I was not responding and therefore my chances were slim.

During this critical time, I had an experience that will stay with me until the day I die. I hesitated to tell anyone about this at first for fear they would think the crack on my head had affected my mind. Believe me, it didn't. I remember seeing a very bright light. It was so bright that the only comparison I might be able to make is when the sun hits a mirror a blinding light shines back and makes it very difficult to look at. In the midst of this bright light there were some beautiful green and red and orange leaves. It was so beautiful and right in the middle of it there was a hand and the hand seemed to be reaching out to me. The hand kept getting closer, closer and closer to me, and I was going toward it. All of a sudden it lifted up as though to stop me. Then all of a sudden the hand started slipping away, backing farther and farther away from me. I truly believe that was the hand of the Lord because they told me that I had been just a breath away from death.

The next thing I remember is opening my eyes and seeing people standing around me. I recognized my husband, but my vision was very blurry. Then to the right I saw a familiar head of blonde-feminine hair standing next to the Roman collar of a priest. The blond hair was Virginia McNiff, Father's assistant, and the priest was Father Ralph. And I remember looking up at his face and trying to say, "Hi, Father." I don't remember if the words came out, but I remember trying. And I knew when I looked up at his face everything was going to be all right because God had sent him there to pray for me, and he did. I also remember my mother staying in touch with me and letting me know how much she loves me.

I remember Father Ralph coming to see me in

intensive care and my husband coming to see me every day of the three weeks I was in that unit.

During that time my daughter had come up to visit me, as she would so many more times. She had been told I could not go to her because I was in an accident and had hurt my leg. They didn't want to tell her how seriously I was injured until they were certain she was well on her way to recovery. I still didn't know how seriously I was hurt, but I know I felt better when I saw my daughter's face. I was so happy.

After intensive care, I was transferred to another unit where they allowed me to sit up and try to move a little. I remember the day when they removed one of the casts from my leg and took the staples out of my skin. Those doctors and nurses were so special, so caring. But through it all, I remember the prayers.

One day a priest came in to bring me Holy Communion. That was a very, very special day for me and I thought, O God, You brought me this far and You gave Your life for me. Now I'm able to partake of You and You are giving Yourself to me again. How unworthy I am! The priests and the lay ministers came every day to bring me Communion.

I owe such a debt to the people in Father's ministry because not a day went by when someone did not come to see me, not one day. They came every day and every evening. I remember another time when I felt very low, then all of a sudden I looked up and there was a clown standing by my bed. Aldona and some other people in the ministry prayer line sent a clown carrying a big bunch of balloons to joke and kid with me. I ask God to bless all my friends and family who came to see me. They were all so special to me. I thank God for my husband who traveled from our home to the hospital every morning, and my daughter who came with her friend the latter part of the day. And I ask God to bless the doctors and nurses, for I never will forget how they treated me so specially.

One of the nurses told a dear friend of mine that I would never walk again. But the therapists in the rehabilitation unit would not give up. They took me into that unit every day and got me standing. After they had accomplished everything with me that was humanly possible, putting my pieces back together like Humpty Dumpty, they helped me learn to sit and stand. Then, the day I was being transferred to Mercy Hospital, my doctor came in and said she had not believed I ever would recover. "We had a lot of help, a lot of help from upstairs," she told me. "Young lady, you are a miracle." As she said that to me, I realized that God's hands had guided her hands and the other doctors' hands in all that they did for me. As the medical staff put me back together, God mended my spiritual life, making it so strong that nothing except God can penetrate my soul.

What I saw when I arrived at the Mercy Hospital rehabilitation facilities was an old dreary building. I thought, Oh, my God, what now? But, you know, inside that building were the nicest, most steadfast people. They refused to give up on me. There were some days that I could not do the things they asked me to. They taught me to slide on a board from my bed to a wheelchair and I thought, "Why are they teaching me this? I want to walk." Many a night I talked to God, asking him if that was what he had in store for me. But then I thought, "No, I am not going to ask, 'Why me?'" I had not asked it up until then and I was not about to start. God had let me live and regardless of the condition I was in, I was alive.

They persisted in that rehab unit. After four months I still had a cast on. Finally, Dr. Clark came in and said he was going to leave it on for a while longer. Learning to walk while wearing the cast was difficult because I could not put weight on the other leg either. Still, the therapists persisted. I was in the University of Massachusetts Hospital for Thanksgiving and for Christmas, and now I was spending New Year's Day in Mercy Hospital. I remember waking up on New Year's Eve and looking out the window. I could see a fireworks display from my bed and I knew that not only was a new year beginning, but a new life and a new time were beginning for me.

After much more work, I was allowed to go home on a weekend pass. After the furniture was rearranged to accommodate my wheelchair, I made my entrance. It was like being born again, being in my home after all those months in the hospital. Actually, it had been four and a half months when the doctor announced I was going home. During all that time, my husband had come to be with me every day, and even pushed me to the dining room so I could eat with the other patients.

I can't explain it any better than to say that the nurses, doctors, and therapists truly are angels of mercy. At times their therapy was more like torture than mercy, but I realize that it was for my own good.

I am walking now. I use a quad cane. I have a rod in my right leg from my knee to my ankle. I have a plate and pins in my left leg from my hip to my knee with about fifteen or sixteen screws in it. I can use my right arm, but my left arm healed on a slant so I can't raise it very high. All my ribs are healed. The hole in the back of my leg has healed. The crack on my head has healed and my hair has grown back. But the biggest healing of all was the healing I had in my love of God. You know, before my accident I went to church on Sunday. I listened to the words of the priest. I went into the prayer house chapel and listened to the teachings. The words had some meaning for me, but now I can truly say how much more meaning they have.

They are the words of God. Now I truly understand what He means when He commands us to love one another. I have learned to forgive my enemies. I had learned to ask God to bless my enemies and to bless all the people who have hurt me. I ask forgiveness from those whom I have hurt. There is no way I can describe how differently and how fully I love people now. Needless to say, I pray for tractor-trailer drivers every day and ask God to keep them safe on their journeys.

Most of all, I have learned that God is alive and that God is there when we need Him. I have never asked, "Why me, Lord?" But now I say, "You saved me. Thank You. You put out Your hand to me, then said, 'No, go back.' " He let me live and maybe that's because He wants me to tell others about His love. I don't know. What I do know is that God loves each of us in a personal, custom-designed way. He will give each of us what we ask for in His time, not ours. I have so many people to thank for all they have done and still do for me, including people who don't even know me, but prayed for me anyway. And I am so thankful to Father Ralph for his prayers on my behalf. I know I was healed by God through Father's love for his fellow human beings. I felt this when he prayed with me.

It was my love, a mother's love, that led to my accident, and only a mother understands that I would go through it again for my daughter and any other member of my family.

PRAYER

My heart cries in tones of joyful gratitude.
You healed my whole life, Lord. Every bone in my
body experienced the atrocity of that almost fatal

destiny. Death was just a step away. Words fail to expound the sentiments branded forever in the wounds of my body and soul.

Lord, my spirit glows! I'm still alive! I'm still in the presence of my loved ones. By Your grace alone I can continue working for You and the pained souls who come to our Apostolate of Prayer.

In gratitude I pray a gentle belief:

"He will not break the bruised reed." (Isaiah 42:3)

"He restores my failing health." (Psalm 23:3)

"Signs and Wonders of Our Time"

Brief accounts of healings

When someone becomes a Christian he becomes a brand new person inside. He is not the same any more. A new life has begun!

All these new things are from God who brought us back to himself through what Christ Jesus did. And God has given us the privilege of urging everyone to come into his favor and be reconciled to him. For God was in Christ, restoring the world to himself, no longer counting men's sins against them but blotting them out. This is the wonderful message he has given us to tell others. (2 Corinthians 5:17–19)

The children, men, and women Jesus heals through me touch me deeply in a way I cannot explain. Sometimes I actually feel their pain and experience their joy. I am always filled with extreme gratitude to God for His healing love, and also feel deep appreciation to God for allowing me to help bring His children closer to Him. Although the initial healing experience may last but a moment, the relationship between God and the individual He has healed is changed forever. Let me tell you briefly about some healings as I experienced them.

———◆———

In August of 1983, I had the privilege of anointing singer Marisa DiMara with holy oil. She had a cataract on her left eye and was told she needed corrective surgery. I prayed over her and then my mother, Molly DiOrio, took Marisa's face in her hands and prayed. During the prayers Marisa felt a warmth cover the side of her face. Afterward she felt peaceful, and a sense of confidence in the Lord. Marisa attended many more healing services and received the complete healing she so actively pursued. As her doctor wrote, "I truly do not understand the great improvement in the vision of your left eye. Today you read the 20/20 line." Since her healing, Marisa has dedicated her voice to the Lord and she praises him in song at many of my healing services.

———◆———

While on pilgrimage to the Holy Land, I had the privilege of praying over Michael J. Gallo of Allentown, New Jersey. A member of our party, Mr. Gallo has diabetes mellitus, a disease in which the body cannot process sugar properly because of insufficient insulin. He was taking a prescribed medicine for diabetics and following a low-calorie, sugar-restricted diet.

I prayed over Mr. Gallo on August 5, 1984, and knew immediately that God had healed him. I told him that he was well, but advised him to continue taking the prescribed medicine until his physician instructed otherwise.

Blood test results sent to me by Mr. Gallo's doctors show an elevated blood sugar count of 212 mg/dl in August of 1983, and a nearly normal level of 155 mg/dl on August 19, 1984, after his healing. His doctor also states that Mr. Gallo now only needs diet therapy.

———◆———

God enjoys working with physicians, as He shows us in this next story. Eunice Ladue attended seven of my healing services before we met. She was sitting in a wheelchair, feeling warm, peaceful, and full of love, when I walked over to her. She told me she had holes in her ankles, then, at my request, stood and walked with me. Mrs. Ladue has scleroderma, a systemic disease that deteriorates body tissue and causes a hardening and thickening of the skin. The disease caused the ulcers in her ankles. Weeks after the service, her physician performed a skin graft, a procedure that frequently fails. Here are his comments: "In all fairness, I must say that I instituted a good preventive program but I cannot, in light of my previous experiences with the ravages of scleroderma, claim that this preventive program would have been anywhere near as successful as Mrs. Ladue's has been. I remain amazed that she has not had any breakdown in two and a half years and furthermore that her skin and grafts look so healthy."

———◆———

On November 2, 1985, I preached God's word to thousands of people in Corpus Christi, Texas. The huge room was filled with the Holy Spirit, and people fell down one after another to rest with Him.

During the service I received the word of knowledge that God was healing six women of emotional trauma caused by rape. I asked them to come to me, but only two or three responded at first. Of course, I understood the hesitation, and continued encouraging the other women to come forth. Some assumed the healing was not for them, and a woman from Arkansas hoped it was not for her. She sat in the bleachers shaking, frightened, not wanting to make her pain known. Suddenly, she felt a tremendous urge to come down to me, but was distracted by the cries of a woman for whom I was praying. Once again she retreated into her fear, then bravely stepped out and started down to join the others who had been called. A fellow priest, seeing that this woman was trembling, took her arm and led her down to the stage. A few minutes later, when I asked her to tell a little bit about what had happened to her, she was relaxed and no longer embarrassed. I asked if she would allow me to anoint her and she calmly answered, "Oh, yes." As I reached my fingers toward her, I felt a surge of electricity, and she fell back to rest with the Holy Spirit. When she awoke she was at peace, healed of the deep ache she had endured for so long.

———◆———

Back in the early days of my healing ministry, I held services in St. John's Church in Worcester. I was still in awe of the gift God had given me, and remember the countless people God healed in that church as though each encounter happened yesterday.

On January 11, 1979, as I called out healings in St. John's Church, heat started moving through the body of a man with rheumatoid arthritis. It started in his toes, traveled up through his back, then seeped into his arms and legs. The religious medal he was wearing felt like it was burning the skin on his chest. I knew a man with arthritis was being healed, and called for him to come forward. Myles Maynard of New York, whose rheumatoid arthritis had been diagnosed eleven years before, claimed his healing. I prayed over him and he told me he felt no pain whatsoever. He said he had trouble walking and I told him, "In the name of Jesus, run!" He ran with ease and remains well today.

One spring evening in 1981, as I walked along the aisle of St. John's Church in Worcester, I placed my hand on the left shoulder of Theresa Hastie, who was under treatment for long-standing hypothyroidism (underactive thyroid). At that moment Jesus healed her, putting an end to a life of overwhelming fatigue and cruel ridicule. It is difficult for observers to distinguish between fatigue and laziness, and some people wrongly judge others. In Theresa Hastie's case, peers, teachers, and even those closest to her had made fun of her because of her lack of energy. An artist who went to school in Dorchester, then at the Boston Museum of Fine Arts, Theresa treasured the understanding love of a few teachers and friends, and forgave the cruelty of others. Since the healing service, to her doctor's surprise, her thyroid tests are normal and she no longer needs medication. A hardworking, self-disciplined woman, she takes care of her elderly mother and ill sister.

As my schedule grows increasingly busy, I spend less and less time at the apostolate office. One day in

May 1986, when I definitely was not planning to go to the apostolate office, I felt compelled to be there and only there. As I walked in the front door, I realized why God had called me to that place. A desperate man sat inside with a prayer counselor. He was confused, anxious, and deeply depressed. He said he could not concentrate even long enough to pray, and saw no reason or purpose to his life. As we talked, he began to feel better. As a priest, my role was to listen, comfort, and guide. In His role, God healed this man of consuming depression. Now he has a job, a smile, and a renewed relationship with his Savior.

◆

When the word of knowledge comes to me, I sometimes perceive the color the afflicted person is wearing. At a service for more than ten thousand people in Cleveland, Ohio, I realized a woman wearing purple was being healed of systemic lupus erythematosus, a chronic disease that deteriorates connective tissue. When I called her out, she was praying intensely for her niece. As I prayed over her, she became warm and started shaking. Since that day in 1983, Isabelle Manzo has been free of all symptoms of lupus, and is considered to be in prolonged remission.

◆

As a member of my ministry, Sister Arlene Lareau prays with the sick and joyfully witnesses healings via the prayer line and healing services. In late summer 1986, Sister Arlene, who has been a nun for her entire adult life, stood in her choir robe in Worcester Memorial Auditorium watching people accept their healings. She had a cataract in her left eye, clouding her sight. When I called out a general healing of the eyes, the room suddenly appeared brighter to her. "It was so vivid, just like someone put the light on," she said later. After God improved the vision in Sister Arlene's eye, her prescription lens was too strong. She went to see her eye doctor who noted the "significant improvement" and ordered a weaker lens.

Rita M. Bergen was one of many people who stood in hopes her hearing would improve at a service in Worcester on June 1, 1986. For about four years Mrs. Bergen could not hear anything with her left ear unless she was wearing two hearing aids. At my direction, she removed her hearing aids and put her fingers into her ears. After I prayed she took her fingers from her ears and heard a loud "pop." She wrote, "I could hear Father DiOrio more clearly than I had all afternoon with my hearing aids in." Hearing tests conducted by her doctor indicate the nerve deafness is about the same, but her ability to discriminate speech improved from 80 to 100 percent. She reports that she no longer wears the aids in her left ear, and her hearing remains improved.

John Locher of Michigan had a smiliar experience in Florida in November 1984 and remains healed today. He writes, "In short, I felt something odd or strange when my fingers were in my ears. I could hear the good father plainer and louder, but I still pondered or doubted until Sunday evening. I kept telling my wife to turn the television down because I felt it was too loud. She told me that for years I could not hear it at that volume level. Praise God!" His doctor reports, "It should be noted that today's [August 27, 1985] test results for the left ear differ significantly from those obtained in 1983. Mr. Locher's hearing seems to have gotten better."

---◆---

During the summer of 1986, I had the privilege of serving the poorest of God's children at several healing services in Castries, St. Lucia, West Indies. God's faithful and hopeful children ventured to services by whatever means available. Some poor, crippled individuals were pushed in wheelbarrows to the meeting places. Mothers and fathers carried their sick children along dirt roads to the hot, crowded buildings. Their faith reached out to Jesus and he showered them with many blessings. A toddler who could not walk now runs around. Thank you, Jesus.

---◆---

I received the word of knowledge that a woman wearing red was being healed of a colon problem at a service in Worcester in the fall of 1982. I asked her to identify herself and an usher brought Barbara Smith of Boston to the stage. She felt a warm sensation in her abdomen and started to perspire as we stood together. Ms. Smith told me she had frequent attacks of abdominal pain and diarrhea, lasting two or three days at a time. She had been diagnosed years before as having a spastic colon, which means the muscles would tense, especially when she was anxious. Ms. Smith's physician had given her a restricted diet because certain foods also caused prolonged episodes of pain and diarrhea.

I told her she had not come to the service because of this infirmity, and she said she came seeking healings for her brother and mother. I anointed her hands with holy oil and she was overcome by the Holy Spirit. When she awoke she was relaxed, a feeling foreign to her until then. Foods that used to cause attacks no longer bother her, and she is a much calmer person now.

Mistrust, rebellion, alcohol, drugs, gambling, and barroom brawling were a way of life for Roger Berube of Palm Bay, Florida, until he made friends with Jesus Christ at a healing service in St. Bernard's Church in Fitchburg. He says, "I had been drinking heavily daily since I was eighteen years old, and my doctor had told me I would be crippled by the time I was forty. I am forty-five now and anyone can see how good my health is. I have not craved nor drunk any alcohol since I accepted Jesus' love for me.

"I went reluctantly to the first meeting. I felt something very different and special about Father Di-Orio, and returned for several more meetings. In September of 1976, while Father was teaching total forgiveness of sins through Jesus, I accepted Jesus as my Savior and Lord, and things have not been the same since. The old life-style was taking and using. In my new life with Jesus I have learned that it is in giving that we receive."

Now a loving husband who enjoys being with his children, Roger has turned 180 degress from the self-destructive path he followed for more than fifteen years. Although he had never sung before, he has started singing God's message more beautifully than words can describe. Roger shares his gift with me and thousands of others at my Worcester services and at other worship meetings.

———◆———

When a son gets married his entire family benefits from the love of a new family member. Occasionally, however, life's complexities cause problems: Walls are built and the families divide. One day, as I walked along the aisles of a healing service, I had the privilege of being used to transmit a family healing. I saw a troubled woman and felt her pain. Filled with God's love for His daughter, I reached out and held her hand and prayed for her. Peace filled her heart and pushed out the pain. She cried all the way home to her husband, who also felt touched by Jesus. Soon afterward, their estranged son invited them both to his home, where his parents had been unwelcome for years. To their extreme joy they saw their granddaughter for the first time. Since that time the love and peace between the parents, their son, daughter-in-law, and grandchild has blossomed and grown.

OTHER IMAGE BOOKS

OTHER IMAGE BOOKS